HAL LEONARD JAZZ PIANO METHOD BOOK 2

The Player's Guide to Authentic Stylings

BY MARK DAVIS

Speed • Pitch • Balance • Loop

To access audio, visit:
www.halleonard.com/mylibrary
Enter Code
7190-1271-2589-8043

ISBN: 978-1-5400-3968-2

Visit Hal Leonard Online at
www.halleonard.com

Contact Us:
Hal Leonard
7777 West Bluemound Road
Milwaukee, WI 53213
Email: info@halleonard.com

In Europe contact:
Hal Leonard Europe Limited
42 Wigmore Street
Marylebone, London, W1U 2RN
Email: info@halleonardeurope.com

In Australia contact:
Hal Leonard Australia Pty. Ltd.
4 Lentara Court
Cheltenham, Victoria, 3192 Australia
Email: info@halleonard.com.au

CONTENTS

INTRODUCTION

The *Hal Leonard Jazz Piano Method Book 2* is a continuation of the *Hal Leonard Jazz Piano Method* (which from now on I will refer to as *JPM*). Intermediate and advanced level jazz pianists may be able to jump in and fully benefit from *Book 2*, but most people will find it extremely useful to pick up a copy of *JPM*, which introduces topics that are further developed here. If you are puzzled by any of the concepts in *Book 2*, you are likely to find explanations of those concepts in *JPM*. Throughout *Book 2*, you will see references to specific pages from *JPM* that can be reviewed for fundamental information.

I hope you are enjoying the process of learning to play jazz piano. Take your time and get comfortable with each concept in this book before moving on. Follow the practice exercises and apply your new skills to repertoire you like to play or are learning. Listen to great recordings and take in live performances. Be curious and be open to new sounds. Anything complex can be broken down into simpler, more manageable components, so analyze what you hear and figure out how you can incorporate new material into your own playing. Share your findings with teachers and fellow musicians, and ask questions of those who know more than you do. The more you learn, the more fun it is to play jazz. Mastering basic techniques that can be combined in an infinite number of ways is what makes improvisation a rewarding lifelong pursuit.

Chapter 1
STRENGTHENING THE BASICS

As you progress in your study of jazz piano and continue to learn complex techniques, you will find that having a solid foundation in fundamentals is vital. This chapter presents ways to continue strengthening the basic skills and theoretical knowledge you have been acquiring.

SEVENTH CHORDS

Here are formulas for the most common types of seventh chords. This information was detailed in *JPM* (page 17) and is provided here as a review. In the table below, the chord symbols use C as the root, but chords can be played in any of the 12 keys. The symbols in bold are the ones I use for subsequent examples in this book.

Major 7th	1 3 5 7	symbols: **Cmaj7**, Cma7, CM7, C△7
Dominant 7th	1 3 5 ♭7	symbol: **C7**
Minor 7th	1 ♭3 5 ♭7	symbols: **Cm7**, Cmin7, Cmi7, C-7
Half-diminished 7th also called Minor 7th(♭5)	1 ♭3 ♭5 ♭7	symbols: **Cø7**, Cø symbols: Cmin7(♭5), Cmi7(♭5), Cm7(♭5), C-7(♭5)
Diminished 7th	1 ♭3 ♭5 ♭♭7	symbol: **C°7**
Minor-major 7th	1 ♭3 5 7	symbols: **Cm(maj7)**, Cmin(maj7), C-(△7)

UPPER EXTENSIONS

Here are formulas for the upper extensions that are most often used with the various seventh chords. This information was detailed in *JPM* (pages 59-60) and is summarized here.

Major 7th	9	♯11	13	
Dominant 7th	9	♯11	13 (also ♭9, ♯9, ♭13)	
Minor 7th	9	11	13	
Half-diminished 7th	9	11	♭13	
Diminished 7th	9	11	♭13	maj7
Minor-major 7th	9	11	13	

SHELL VOICINGS

A shell voicing contains just the root, 3rd, and 7th (or 6th) of a chord. There are two types of shell voicings: closed and open. This information was detailed in *JPM* (pages 18-22).

Here is how to play a closed-shell voicing.

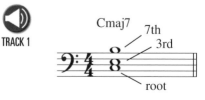

The 3rd and 7th can be flatted as needed to create the various chord qualities, or the 6th can be used in place of the 7th. Here are examples of various chord qualities played with closed-shell voicings.

TRACK 2

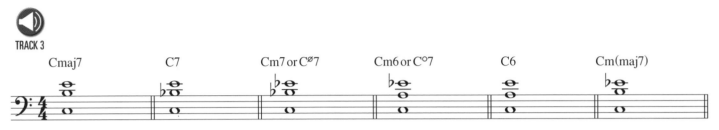

To play an open-shell voicing, start with a closed-shell voicing and move the 3rd up an octave to create a voicing that spans a 10th. The following example shows how to play various chord qualities with open-shell voicings.

TRACK 3

ADDING NOTES TO SHELL VOICINGS

The next 24 examples (Tracks 4-27) will strengthen your harmonic understanding and acquaint you with voicings that can be used for comping or harmonizing melodies. Throughout the examples, I adhere to a set of guidelines for adding one or two notes to shell voicings that will allow you to create four- and five-note voicings. There are many other possibilities, but the following guidelines will get you started playing some useful chord voicings. (*JPM*, pages 60-62, introduces two-handed voicings.)

Guidelines for Adding Notes to a *Closed Shell:*

Create a four-note voicing by adding the 9th on top. (If the chord is a dominant 7th, additional options are ♭9th or ♯9th.)

For a second note, add the 5th on top (above the 9th) or within the voicing to create a five-note voicing. (With dominant 7th chords, it is common to add the 13th or ♭13th instead of the 5th.)

Here are a few examples of closed-shell voicings with one or two notes added to each. I used chord symbols that show which extensions have been included. Cmaj9 indicates a major 7th chord with the 9th added, Cm9 is a minor 7th chord with the 9th added, and C9 is a C7 chord with the 9th added. The numbers next to the notes correspond to notes of a major scale (in this case C major) and are provided to help you transpose these chords to other keys.

TRACK 4

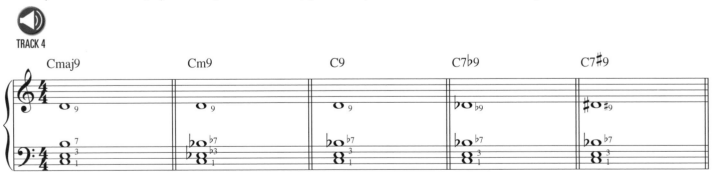

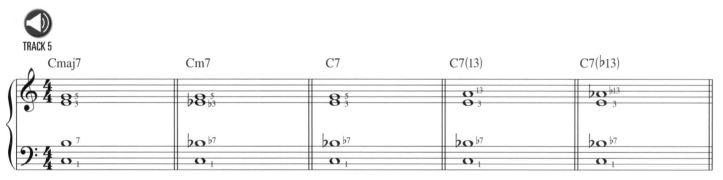

Guidelines for Adding Notes to an *Open Shell:*

Create a four-note voicing by adding the 5th on top. (If the chord is a dominant 7th, it is common to add the 13th or ♭13th instead of the 5th. Adding the 13th, instead of the 5th, to major 7th chords works well, too.)

For a second note, add the 9th on top (above the 5th) or within the voicing (between the 7th and the 3rd) to create a five-note voicing. (Additional options with dominant 7th chords are ♭9th or ♯9th.)

Here are some examples of open-shell voicings with one or two notes added.

TRACK 5

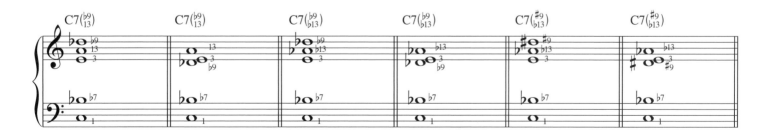

Practice: Learn to play each voicing from Tracks 4 and 5 in all keys, moving through the cycle of fourths (*JPM*, page 13).

TWO-HANDED VOICING EXERCISES

The next 11 exercises (Tracks 6-16) involve an alternating sequence of open- and closed-shell voicings with one more note added to each to create four-note, two-handed voicings. These are followed by 11 exercises (Tracks 17-27) that involve an alternating sequence of open and closed shells with *two* more notes added to each, creating five-note, two-handed voicings. For simplicity, I used chord symbols that don't include extensions. Learn to play each exercise from memory.

In the first of these exercises, I play major 7th chords through the cycle and alternate between an open shell with the 5th added on top and a closed shell with the 9th added on top.

The following exercise is the same as Track 6, but everything is a half step higher so that all the chords that were closed in the preceding example are now open, and the chords that were open are now closed.

It's important to incorporate rhythm into your practice. In the following example, I play the preceding two exercises with syncopated rhythms I might use when comping. Notice that I play with a swing feel. Learn to play this example, and then apply these types of rhythms to the subsequent exercises in this section.

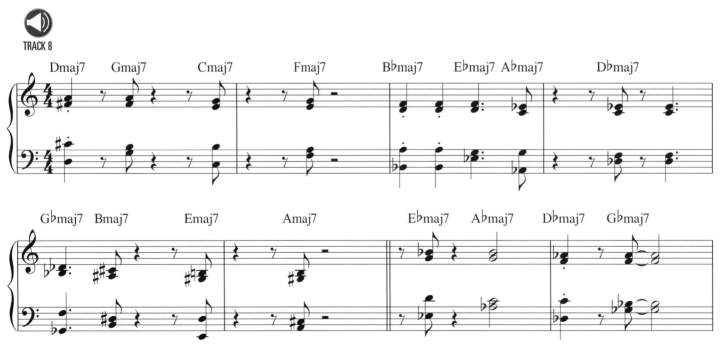

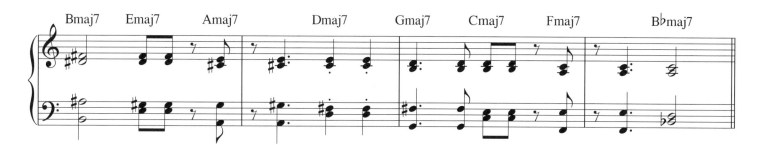

In the next exercise, I play minor 7th chords through the cycle and alternate between an open shell with the 5th added on top and a closed shell with the 9th added on top.

Now try it up a half step.

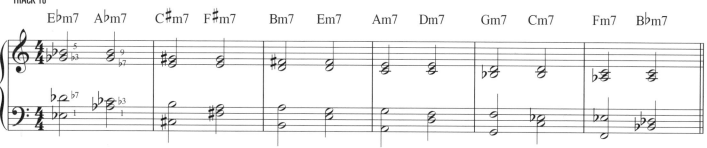

Now play dominant 7th chords through the cycle and alternate between an open shell with the 13th added on top and a closed shell with the 9th added on top.

Here is the same dominant 7th exercise up a half step.

TRACK 12

You can play the previous two exercises and include altered extensions. The 9th can be replaced with the ♭9th or ♯9th, and the 13th can be replaced by the ♭13th or the 5th. The following four examples will acquaint you with some of the possibilities. After you have learned these, play them a half step higher. In the first of these examples, I alternate between adding the ♭13th and the 9th.

TRACK 13

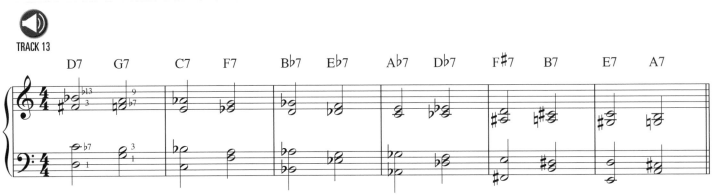

Next, I alternate between adding the ♭13th and the ♯9th to dominant 7th chords.

TRACK 14

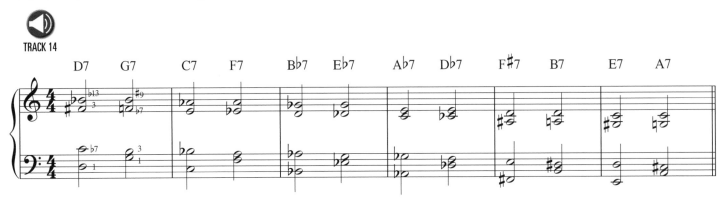

This exercise alternates between adding the 5th and the ♭9th to dominant 7th chords.

TRACK 15

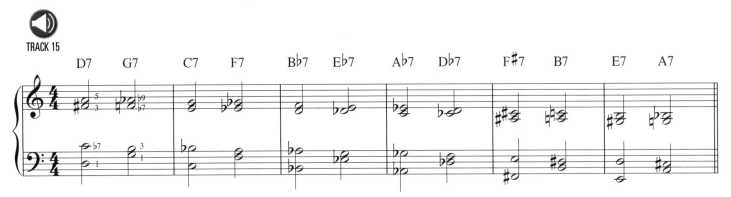

This one alternates between adding the 5th and the ♯9th to dominant 7th chords.

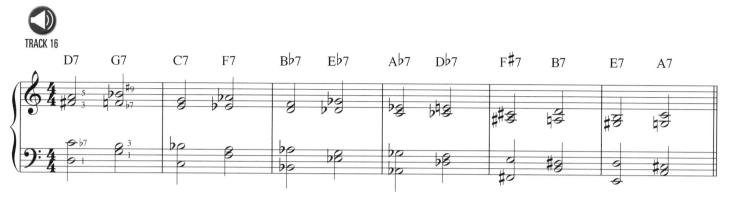

In the following exercise, I add two notes to each shell voicing to create five-note voicings. I play major 7th chords through the cycle and alternate between an open shell and closed shell with the 5th and 9th added to each. After you can play this, learn to play it a half step higher.

Here is the same exercise, but with the 9th applied to the open shell in a different position and the 5th applied to the closed shell in a different position. After you can play this, learn to play it a half step higher.

Here I play a similar exercise to Track 17, but this time with minor 7th chords. After you can play this, learn to play it a half step higher.

Here is the same exercise as Track 19, but with the 9th applied to the open shell in a different position and the 5th applied to the closed shell in a different position. After you can play this, learn to play it a half step higher.

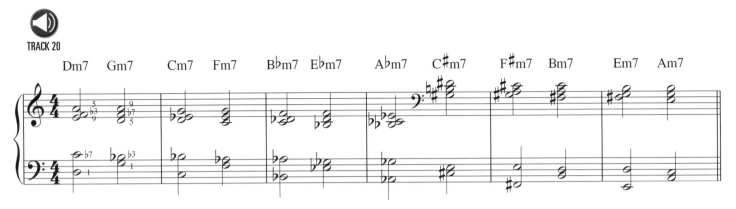

Next, I play dominant 7th chords and alternate between open and closed shells with the 9th and 13th added to each. After you can play this, learn to play it a half step higher.

Here is the same exercise but with the 9th applied to the open shell in a different position and the 13th applied to the closed shell in a different position. After you can play this, learn to play it a half step higher.

Now try the previous two exercises with altered extensions included. The 9th can be replaced by the ♭9th or ♯9th, and the 13th can be replaced by the ♭13th or the 5th. The following three examples demonstrate just a few of the possibilities. After you can play these, learn to play them a half step higher.

Here are some examples of these five-note voicings applied to a iim7–V7–Imaj7 progression. Learn to play these in all keys.

Here are examples of just some of the ways you can include altered dominant 7th voicings in the iim7–V7–Imaj7 progression. Learn to play these in all keys.

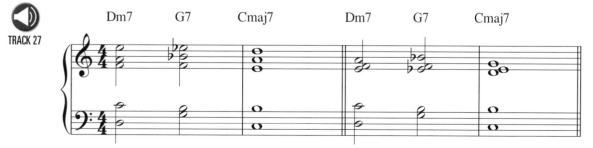

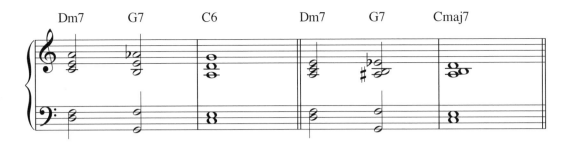

Practice: The main purpose of the exercises presented thus far is to further your harmonic understanding, so learn to play each exercise from memory. Apply the types of rhythms used in Track 8 to all the exercises. Use a metronome set to click on beats 2 and 4 or play with an accompaniment track. You might use a computer or phone app that provides drum loops that will allow you to practice with a swing feel, Latin feel, or other groove. There are a lot of exercises here, so make a few a part of your daily practice. Master each one before moving on. This may take a while, so it can be an ongoing project as you continue to work on other things.

MELODIC EXERCISES

The 3rd and 7th of a chord are important notes in determining its quality and are sometimes referred to as **guide tones*** because they can be used to guide a listener's ear through a harmonic progression. Guide tones can be played simultaneously to create harmony, as in the upper two notes of the shell voicings, or they can be played in succession to create a **guide tone line.** In the following example, I create a guide tone line using the 3rds and 7ths of dominant 7th chords that move through the cycle. I achieve a smooth flow by using the 7th of each chord to lead to the 3rd of the next chord.

TRACK 28

In the next example, I use notes of the dominant scale to fill in between the two guide tones to create a longer idea. In the first measure of the example, I play down the scale from the 3rd to the 7th. In the second measure, I play the same scale segment but shift up an octave after the first note. Barry Harris, the master jazz pianist and educator, calls this technique of shifting up an octave during a descending scale run, "**pivoting.**" This is a good way to keep a line from getting too low, and the octave shift creates a more interesting line. The 3rd and 7th measures of the melody of Kenny Dorham's composition "Blue Bossa" are good examples of how effective this pivot technique can be.

TRACK 29

*The terms in bold are defined in the glossary.

Here I use the ideas from Track 29 to play a line over a cycle of dominant 7th chords. The bridge of Duke Jordan's composition "Jordu" is a good place to try playing lines like these.

TRACK 30

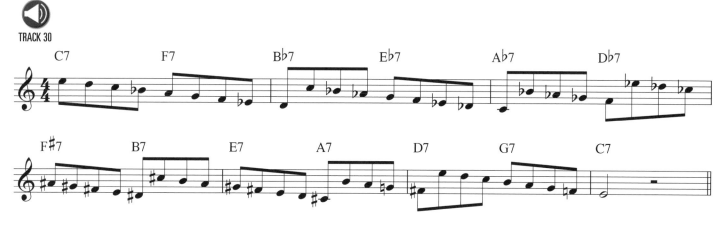

You can use **chord tones** to fill in between the two guide tones. Here are a couple of ways to do that.

TRACK 31

Here's a line over a cycle of dominant 7th chords that uses the ideas from Track 31.

TRACK 32

The following example uses the chord progression of the A section of "Autumn Leaves," but with a faster **harmonic rhythm**. There are two chords per measure rather than one chord per bar as in the original. I demonstrate how the techniques presented in Tracks 29-32 can be applied to a progression that contains chords of various qualities.

TRACK 33

Practice: The melodic exercises in this chapter are designed to hone your **chops**, and at the same time sharpen the mental skills you need to improvise. Become fluent with these exercises and apply the techniques presented in Tracks 30 and 32 to other chord qualities. Practice using these techniques over the progression from Track 33 and then learn to play this exercise in the other keys.

Chapter 2
EXPANDING YOUR MELODIC VOCABULARY

In *JPM*, I introduced you to scales, arpeggios, and other melodic ideas that can be used to create improvisations. In this chapter, we'll look at ways to expand this melodic vocabulary.

EXTENDED ARPEGGIOS

Here is an example of three four-note arpeggios connected by G7 bebop scale segments. (I covered these techniques in *JPM*, pages 39-43.) The arpeggios begin on the 3rd, 5th, and 7th of G7 and connect to the root, 3rd, and 5th, respectively. Remember that the dominant bebop scale and related material can be played over the related ii-7 as well as the related viiø7; e.g., you can play the G7 bebop scale and related material over G7, Dmin7, and Bø7. (See *JPM*, page 76, for an explanation of how to use a dominant bebop scale over a half-diminished chord.)

TRACK 34

Five-note arpeggios can be formed by extending each four-note arpeggio up another 3rd. Notice in the following example that the final note of the arpeggio now lands *on* the beat, so I descend from the 4th, 6th, and root of G7 and include additional notes to get back on track with chord tones landing on the beat. (See *JPM*, page 41, to review descending dominant bebop scales.) Playing five-note arpeggios is tricky, so I've included a couple of fingering possibilities. Experiment to find what works best for you.

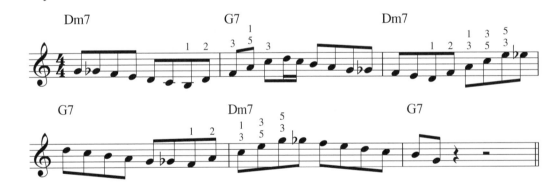

TRACK 35

Charlie Parker liked to play the arpeggio from the 3rd of the dominant and leap all the way up to the 13th. Here is an example of that with a couple of fingering options.

TRACK 36

Practice: Learn to play extended arpeggios in all the keys. Figure out how you learn best. You might choose to play each of these tracks in all keys, moving through the cycle. Or you might choose to practice one arpeggio at a time, and work on including it in your improvisations. Practice in tempo and use a metronome or accompaniment track to help strengthen your sense of time.

REVERSE DIRECTION ARPEGGIOS

You can reverse the direction of the dominant arpeggios. Here are the same three arpeggios used in Track 34, but this time I play them descending, followed by the note that might come after each one.

The reverse direction (descending) arpeggios begin with notes that don't typically fall on the beat in the dominant bebop scale so, to connect the scale to the arpeggios in the following example, I precede the first two arpeggios with an additional passing tone (APT) and use enclosure to connect to the final arpeggio. (I'll cover more about enclosure later in this chapter.)

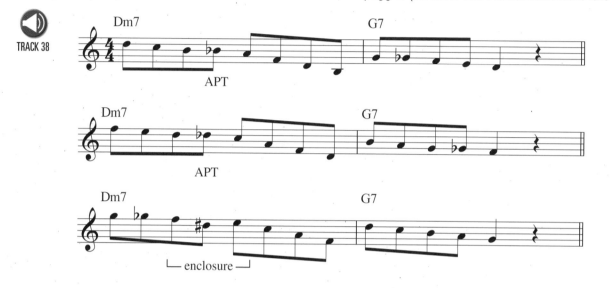

Practice: Experiment with different ways of connecting reverse direction arpeggios to scales and other ideas, and practice including them in your improvisations.

ADDING EMBELLISHMENTS TO SCALES

It's common for jazz musicians to include embellishments when playing a descending scale (or scale segment) of eighth notes. Here is the G7 bebop scale with examples of 16th-note embellishments. Notice that each embellishment consists of a chord tone, followed by a note above, the chord tone again, and a note below.

Often these types of embellishments are notated and played using 16th-note triplets followed by an eighth note. Keep in mind that when playing with a swing feel, the eighth notes will be played with a long-short rhythm. This means that the 16th-note triplets fit into the duration of the longer swing-eighth note and the eighth note that follows is the shorter swing-eighth note. Here is how Track 39 would be notated using 16th-note triplets.

At fast tempos, the rhythm used in Track 39 and the rhythm used in Track 40 will be virtually indistinguishable. At slower tempos, there is more variety among jazz pianists as to how these embellishments are played. Some play four 16th notes, some include the 16th-note triplets, and some play other variations. Listen to the great pianists (at slow speed, if possible) to analyze the different approaches. For the remainder of the embellishment examples, I have chosen to notate with four 16th notes, allowing you to supply the rhythmic nuance.

Here is the G7 bebop scale, the C major bebop scale, and the bebop version of the A7 Jewish (or Spanish) scale with embellishments beginning on chord tones. (See *JPM*, pages 52-53, for more about the major bebop scale and *JPM*, page 74, for more about the Jewish scale.)

When improvising a solo, use these embellishments here and there to add rhythmic interest.

Embellishments can also begin on upper extensions. Let's start with this phrase over iim7–V7–Imaj7. Over G7, I used four notes from a diminished scale. (For more on the diminished scale, see *JPM*, pages 79-82.)

Here is how the phrase from Track 43 can be played with embellishments. Notice that the embellishment over Dmin7 begins on its 9th, the embellishment over G7 begins on its #11th, and the embellishment over Cmaj7 begins on its 9th.

Practice: Play scales in all keys and add embellishments. As with all exercises, experiment with different fingerings until you find what works best.

ADDING EMBELLISHMENTS TO ARPEGGIOS AND INTERVALS

Descending melodic intervals and descending arpeggios can also be embellished. Check out these examples in which I play an eighth-note phrase and then show how it can be embellished.

TRACK 45

Practice: Experiment with lines you typically play and figure out how you can add embellishments.

ENCLOSURES

The melodic technique of leading to a chord tone or other **target note** by using notes that chromatically or diatonically surround it is known as enclosure. I introduced this technique in *JPM*, pages 44-45, as a useful way to connect from one scale to another, but now we'll look at ways it can be used to create melodic interest within a line.

Here's an example of an enclosure that targets the 3rd of the G7 scale. Notice that the **surround tones,** the notes that surround the target note, are from the dominant scale (Mixolydian mode) and have not been chromatically altered. (For more on the Mixolydian mode, see *JPM*, pages 34-35.) For this reason, we can describe this enclosure as diatonic.

TRACK 46

Here's a short idea that incorporates this enclosure.

TRACK 47

Here is the same enclosure idea from Track 46, but this time the surround tones are reversed.

TRACK 48

Here are some ideas that incorporate this enclosure.

Here is a melodic line that includes the ideas from Tracks 47 and 49 applied over a repeated iim7–V7 progression.

Here is an example of an enclosure that targets the 7th of the G7 scale. Notice that the surround tones are again from the dominant scale (Mixolydian mode) and have not been chromatically altered, so the enclosure is diatonic.

Here's a short idea that incorporates this enclosure.

Here is the same enclosure idea, but with the surround tones reversed.

Here are some ideas that incorporate this enclosure.

Here's a melodic line that includes the ideas from Tracks 52 and 54 applied over a repeated iim7–V7 progression.

Here's an enclosure idea that first targets the third note and then the second note of the G7 scale.

Here's a line that includes this idea a couple of times.

When using an enclosure to target the 5th of a dominant scale, we often raise the lower surround tone so that it is a half step below the target note. This creates a strong pull toward the 5th.

Here's how I would use these enclosures following each of the three dominant arpeggios from Track 34.

Here are some more dominant ideas that include enclosures that target the 5th.

TRACK 60

Here's a line that includes enclosure ideas that target the 5th of a dominant scale.

TRACK 61

Using a **chromatic approach note** to lead up to the first note of the enclosures presented in Tracks 46 and 51, and of the first enclosure in Track 58, is another way to create melodic interest. In the following example, I begin on an upbeat and approach enclosures that target the 7th, 5th, and 3rd of a dominant scale from a half step below.

TRACK 62

Here I follow a G7 bebop scale segment with all three ideas back-to-back and then reconnect to the scale. You might not use all three in a row when improvising, but this is an efficient way to practice them.

TRACK 63

Here's how I might use each of these ideas in a musical phrase.

TRACK 64

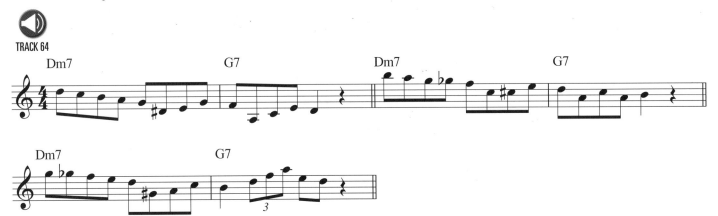

In this variation, each dominant enclosure is preceded by a chromatic approach note that begins *on* the beat rather than on an upbeat.

Here I use these ideas in musical phrases.

Another possibility when using an enclosure to target the 3rd of a dominant scale is to raise the lower surround tone so that it is a half step below the target note like we did when targeting the 5th (see Track 58). This creates a stronger pull toward the 3rd. Similarly, when targeting the first note of a dominant scale, the lower surround note can be raised by a half step.

Enclosures with a lower surround note that is a half step below the target note, can also be applied to major chords. Here are enclosures that target the root, 3rd, and 5th of Cmaj7 or Cmaj6.

Here are some phrases that make use of these enclosures.

You can use a chromatic approach note to lead up to the first note of an enclosure that targets the root or the 5th of a major chord. Here are examples starting both on the upbeat and on the beat.

Here are these ideas included in musical phrases.

It's also possible to chromatically enclose chord tones. The following example shows how you can enclose chord tones of dominant 7th and major chords by using surround tones that are a half step above and a half step below the target note.

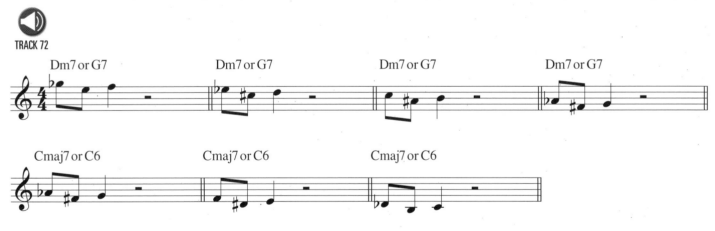

Here's a way to practice the chromatic enclosures from Track 72 by embedding them into a scale.

Here I have included the chromatic enclosures from Track 72 in an improvisation over a repeated iim7–V7–Imaj7.

The chromatic enclosures can be combined with the first two enclosures from Track 62 and the enclosures from Track 70 that begin on an upbeat (measures 1, 2, 4, 5 below). In measure 3, I combined a "resolution to the 3rd" idea (*JPM*, page 43) with the third enclosure from Track 62 to target the 3rd.

Here are how the ideas from Track 75 can be included in phrases from Tracks 64 and 71.

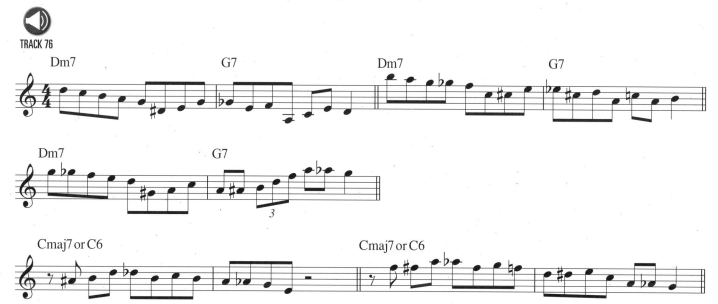

Practice: There is a lot of enclosure material here. Work slowly and methodically. Each idea can open up many possibilities when you're improvising, so pick an idea you like and practice it in all the keys, and then experiment with ways to include it in your solos.

CHROMATIC APPROACH NOTES

In this chapter, we have been using chromatic approach notes in conjunction with enclosures. Here are some ways you can use chromatic approach notes preceding the arpeggios from Track 34.

Here I use chromatic approach notes to precede arpeggios that can be used over major chords.

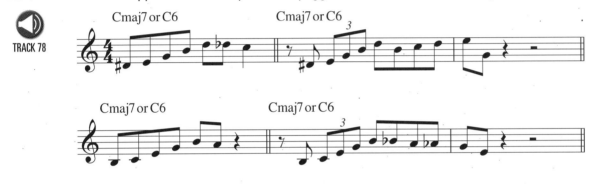

Here are a couple more ideas that start with a chromatic approach note that can be used over a major chord.

Here is a line that includes ideas from Tracks 78 and 79.

Precede diatonic triad arpeggios with chromatic approach notes to create a pattern. Listen to the opening of McCoy Tyner's solo on "Speak Low" from his album *Inception* for a great example of how this technique can be used over a repeated iim7–V7. Here is the pattern in the key of C.

Here are a few ways to include some of the arpeggios with chromatic approach notes from Tracks 79 and 81 in musical phrases.

TRACK 82

Practice: Include chromatic approach note ideas in your solos. Although practicing a particular phrase in all keys by moving through the cycle is an excellent exercise, you may find that spending your time figuring out how to include a phrase in your improvisation over a tune can produce even better, more immediate results. Think of tunes you know that include iim7–V7–Imaj7s, for example. Come up with a list of tunes that, among them, account for iim7–V7–Imaj7s in most, if not all, the keys. This will allow you to practice certain phrases in different keys in a musical context.

MOVING 7th LICKS

If you've played the blues heads "Tenor Madness" by Sonny Rollins or "Billie's Bounce" by Charlie Parker, then you're familiar with a type of musical phrase I call a "moving 7th lick." It occurs in measures 9-10 of these tunes. It is based on a variation of the iim7–V7 progression that involves four chords instead of just two. The expanded progression is iim–iim(maj7)–iim7–V7, and can substitute for a regular iim7–V7. Here is an example of the progression.

TRACK 83

Phrases that are played over the progression in Track 83 are called moving 7th licks because of the way the 7th of the minor-major 7th chord moves down a half step to the 7th of the minor 7th chord and finally down another half step to the 3rd of the dominant 7th chord. Here are some classic moving 7th licks.

TRACK 84

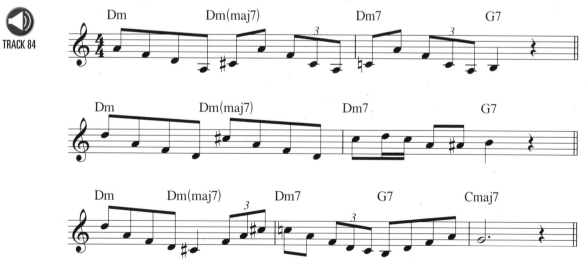

Here are a couple more moving 7th licks that move through the progression more quickly.

Practice: Think of tunes you can play that include iim7–V7s and play moving 7th licks over those measures.

BLUES VOCABULARY

In *JPM*, page 29, you learned that the blues scale is a minor pentatonic scale with the ♭5th added. In addition to improvising with the blues scale over a blues progression, you can use it when improvising over tunes or sections of tunes that are in a minor key. Here is an improvisation that uses the F blues scale over the chords of the A section of Bobby Timmons's composition "Moanin'."

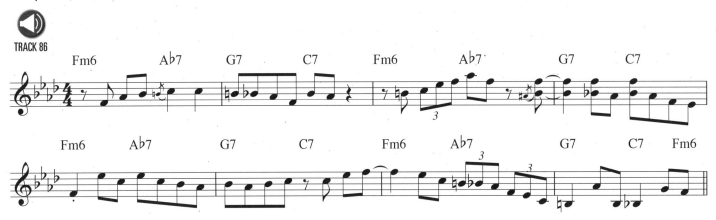

A **major pentatonic scale** is a five-note scale that is composed of the 1st, 2nd, 3rd, 5th, and 6th degrees of a major scale. A major pentatonic scale contains the same notes as a minor pentatonic scale that begins three half steps below. For example, the F major pentatonic scale contains the same notes as the D minor pentatonic scale.

Playing a major pentatonic scale with the ♭3rd added is another way to achieve a bluesy sound. This creates a major version of the blues scale that can be used when improvising on the blues or when improvising over tunes or sections of tunes that are in a major key. Here is the F major version of the blues scale (derived from F major pentatonic) and the D blues scale (derived from D minor pentatonic). Notice that they share the same notes.

Here is an improvisation on an F blues using the F major version of the blues scale over the whole progression. To better fit with the scale and to enhance the bluesy approach, I used F7 in measures 7 and 11 rather than Fmaj7 and used G7 in place of Gm7 in measures 9 and 12. I avoided playing A♮ over B♭7 because it would clash harmonically.

TRACK 89

When playing over a dominant 7th chord, a bluesy sound can be achieved by including the ♭3rd and the ♭5th along with notes from the related dominant scale (Mixolydian mode). Here are some phrases I might play over F7 using this approach.

TRACK 90

Practice: Many of the greatest jazz pianists were masters of incorporating the blues. Oscar Peterson, Horace Silver, and Herbie Hancock are just a few who had distinctive approaches to this. Listen to them and others, and use the ideas from this section to give your playing some soul.

LEARNING BY EAR AND TRANSCRIBING

Listening to jazz and attempting to imitate what you hear is essential to you as a developing jazz musician. Doing so will help you strengthen fundamental skills and assimilate new vocabulary. Notating music you learn by ear is referred to as transcribing, and a written piece of music that is the result of this process is called a transcription. Writing out a solo or harmonic passage, however, should be the final step. First learn to play a phrase or a solo by ear and be able to accurately play it from memory before attempting to notate it. This will strengthen your ears and your ability to memorize. Once you have learned to play something by ear, notating it can be instructive and make analysis easier.

Picking out solos and voicings by ear is difficult for everyone at first, but it gets easier the more you do it. Here are some of the benefits:

- Develops your aural skills (your *ears*, man!)
- Improves your technique
- Strengthens your sense of time and rhythmic feel
- Sharpens your musical memory
- Hones your music notation skills (if you notate what you learn by ear)

- Increases your understanding of theoretical concepts
- Helps you develop a personal style

Choose a player to study. Learning from another pianist is easier in many ways, but studying musicians who play a different instrument can be beneficial as well. Charlie Parker, the great alto saxophonist, is one of the most important and influential improvisers in the history of jazz. Studying his solos and learning **Bird** heads is an important part of a jazz education.

Learn as much as you can about the musician you choose and listen to important recordings he or she made. By focusing on one player for a substantial amount of time, you will begin to figure out their particular techniques and systems of improvisation. You will notice that they play certain ideas on more than one recording. This will help you determine which ideas are the most significant and how you can incorporate them into your own playing. Here are some reasons for choosing a musician to study:

- You admire the musician's playing.
- The artist is significant and influential.
- The technical demands of trying to emulate the player are appropriate to your level.
- The repertoire of the artist includes standard tunes you know or would like to learn.
- The style of the player is relevant to yours or represents a style different from your own, but one you would like to examine.

If you feel that learning music by ear is a daunting task, start with just a short phrase you hear on a recording. You can work your way up to learning a whole chorus or an entire solo. Figuring out chord voicings is generally more difficult than hearing melodic lines, so save harmonic passages until you have more experience with melodic lines. If you study a piano solo, start by picking one that involves linear right-hand lines. If you are able, figure out the left-hand comping, but if that's too difficult in the beginning, simply add your own left-hand voicings based on the chord progression of the tune.

Here are some tips on learning and transcribing solos:

- Pick a solo that's not too difficult.
- Learn the chord progression the solo is based upon.
- Listen to the solo many times using headphones or good quality speakers.
- Learn to sing along with the solo.
- Figure out small sections – even one note at a time if necessary.
- If you're having trouble, slow down the recording using a computer or phone app.
- Don't get hung up on a difficult passage. Get as close as you can and move on.
- Memorize the solo before trying to notate it.
- Try to imitate every nuance as you play the solo.

Here is a list of some solos that are not technically difficult and would be a good place to start:

- Horace Silver's solo on "Song for My Father," from his album *Song for My Father*
- Horace Silver's solo on "Solar," from Miles Davis's album *Walkin'*
- Horace Silver's solo on "Walkin'," from Miles Davis's album *Walkin'*
- Miles Davis's solo on "So What," from his album *Kind of Blue*
- Miles Davis's solo on "Freddie Freeloader," from his album *Kind of Blue*
- First chorus of Red Garland's solo on "Bye, Bye, Blackbird," from Miles Davis's album *'Round About Midnight*

It takes a lot of work to learn to play solos by ear, but it really pays off. Here are some ideas for what to do once you have learned a passage or an entire solo by ear:

- Continue to practice with the original recording.
- Use a computer or phone app that allows you to practice with the original recording at different tempos. If the original tempo is too fast, start with a more comfortable tempo and work your way up.
- Practice the solo with a metronome, accompaniment track, or actual rhythm section.

- Notate the solo and analyze how the lines relate to the chord progression. Identify scales, arpeggios, and other melodic devices.
- Pick out short phases you would like to incorporate into your own playing. Try to break down lines into the smallest vocabulary units that make sense. Transpose this material into other keys and practice inserting these ideas into your solos.
- Compose a solo using vocabulary gleaned from the transcription. This can serve as an etude that you can transpose to other keys.
- Improvise in the style of the solo and include newly learned phrases and vocabulary.

Practice: Figuring out music by ear and transcribing is time consuming, but many jazz musicians consider it to be the most important thing a developing player can do. Make this a significant part of your practice time.

Chapter 3
CHORD PROGRESSIONS AND SUBSTITUTIONS

Becoming familiar with common chord progressions makes learning new tunes much easier. It is also important to start learning some of the **chord substitutions (chord subs)** that can be used to transform a basic progression into something unique and more interesting. Composers use chord substitutions to generate new progressions, as do jazz musicians when they arrange tunes. Musicians will even toss in chord subs on the fly while improvising..

SUBSTITUTING iiim7 FOR Imaj7

Many jazz standards make use of the Imaj7–vim7–iim7–V7 progression. (See *JPM*, page 56.) Here is Imaj7–vim7–iim7–V7 in the key of C played with a combination of closed- and open-shell voicings.

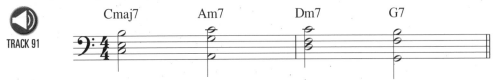

It's common to substitute iiim7 for Imaj7. Here I use the progression from Track 91 and play Em7(iiim7) in place of Cmaj7(Imaj7).

Beginning improvisers sometimes assume that any minor 7th chord is iim7 and therefore use the Dorian mode to improvise over it. (For more about the Dorian mode, see *JPM*, pages 37-38.) The fact is that a minor 7th chord is not always iim7, and instead might be functioning as iiim7 or vim7. Improvise over iiim7 or vim7 with a major scale or major bebop scale as if they were Imaj7. In the following example, I improvise over Em7 and Am7 using the C major bebop scale and related material.

The same concept applies when forming voicings. Although the basic extensions for a minor 7th chord are the 9th, 11th, and 13th, when forming voicings for iiim7, the 9th and the 13th are often avoided, and when forming voicings for vim7, the 13th is often avoided because these notes are outside of the key center (i.e., outside of the major scale from which the iiim7 and vim7 are derived). Here I play Imaj7–vim7–iim7–V7 followed by iiim7–vim7–iim7–V7 and use appropriate extensions.

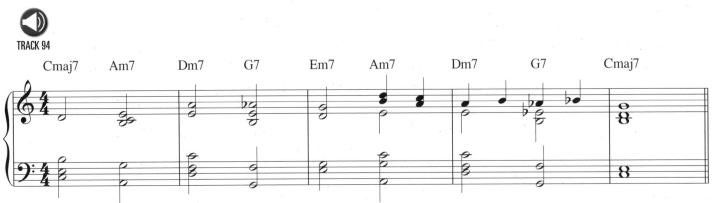

Practice: Learn to play Imaj7–vim7–iim7–V7 and iiim7–vim7–iim7–V7 in all keys using shell voicings and rootless voicings. (For more about rootless voicings, see *JPM*, pages 64-69.) Add notes to the shell voicings to form four- or five-note voicings.

SECONDARY DOMINANTS

In *JPM*, pages 22-23, you learned about the diatonic chords that can be generated from the major scale. There is only one dominant 7th chord (V7) that can be formed using the notes of a major scale. A dominant 7th chord typically **resolves** to a chord that is down a 5th (or up a 4th). That means that in the key of C, G7 is often followed by Cmaj7. It is possible, however, to "borrow" dominant 7th chords from other keys. This allows us to use dominant 7th chords to resolve down a 5th (up a 4th) to diatonic chords other than the **tonic chord**. A dominant 7th chord used in this manner is called a **secondary dominant.** Check out this example.

Notice, in the example above, that I used A7 in place of Am7. A7 is a secondary dominant. It resolves to Dm7 and functions as the V7 of iim7. In the following example, I use secondary dominant 7th chords as subs for the iim7, iiim7, and vim7.

Here I add notes that include extensions to the progression from Track 96. You can hear how much interest the secondary dominants provide.

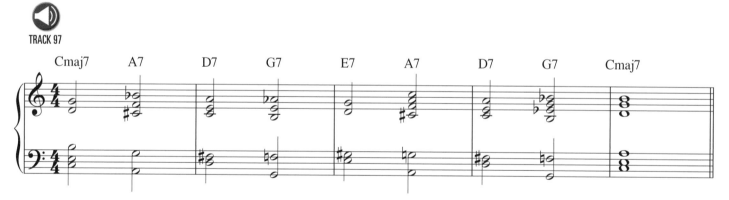

Practice: Learn to play these progressions in all keys. Try adding notes to shell voicings to create more complex harmonies and figure out ways to play these progressions using rootless voicings.

THE TRITONE SUB

One of the best-known chord substitutions is the **tritone substitution (tritone sub)**. It involves replacing a dominant 7th chord with another dominant 7th chord that is a tritone (three whole steps) away. For example, I might substitute D♭7 for G7. This works primarily because they share the same guide tones – the 3rd and 7th of one of the chords is the 7th and 3rd of the other. The 3rd of G7 is B and the 7th of D♭7 is C♭, which is the enharmonic equivalent of B. F is the 7th of G7 and the 3rd of D♭7. Here I play G7 as an open-shell voicing and D♭7 as a closed-shell voicing to demonstrate the similarity between the two chords.

TRACK 98

A tritone sub is most often used in place of a dominant 7th chord that is followed by a chord that is down a 5th (up a 4th). Here I use the tritone sub in the context of a iim7–V7–Imaj7 in C. In this example, Dm7–G7–Cmaj7 has become Dm7–D♭7–Cmaj7 (iim7–♭II7–Imaj7).

TRACK 99

If I add notes that include extensions with the right hand, it can sound like this.

TRACK 100

Practice: Play iim7–♭II7–Imaj7 in all keys. Add notes to create more complex voicings. Although the ♭9th, ♯9th, and ♭13th can be added to a tritone sub, the 9th, ♯11th, and 13th are more commonly used.

DIAGRAM OF CHORD SUBS

There are many ways you can vary the Imaj7–vim7–iim7–V7 progression by applying the chord substitutions you have learned about so far. Take a look at the diagram below. Moving from left to right, choose one chord from each column to create one of 72 possible progressions. You might be surprised by some of the substitutions. For example, you could substitute B♭7 for Cmaj7. To arrive at this requires several steps. B♭7 is a tritone sub for E7, E7 is a secondary dominant used in place of Em7, and Em7 (iiim7) can be used in place of Cmaj7 (Imaj7).

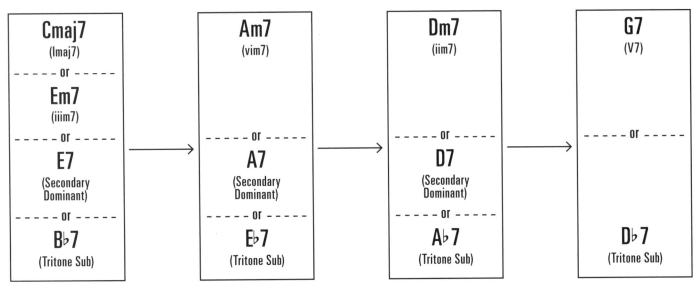

Jazz musicians sometimes **reharmonize** tunes by choosing from these types of chord subs. Let's start with this simple melody over a repeated Imaj7–vim7–iim7–V7 progression.

Here I have reharmonized this melody using chord subs, being careful to choose chords that still fit harmonically with the melody. I added some notes to the shell voicings to fill out the harmonies.

Sometimes a chord sub is inserted between two chords in a progression, serving as a **passing chord**. In the following example, I show how passing chords can be added to a Imaj7–vim7–iim7–V7 progression. Rather than using subs for the entire duration of each chord, I retain the original chords and follow each with a passing chord that leads to the next chord from a half step above. Sometimes this type of passing chord is referred to as a **chromatic approach chord** because it moves to a chord that is a half step away.

Practice: Use the Diagram of Chord Subs to create variations of Imaj7–vim7–iim7–V7. Practice these variations in all keys. Analyze tunes you play and identify where these techniques have been used. Experiment to see where you can add passing chords or substitute chords to tunes in your repertoire.

EXPANDING DOMINANTS: iim7–V7 IN PLACE OF V7

A dominant 7th chord can be thought of as the V7 of a particular key. A common way to expand this chord into two chords is to replace it with a iim7–V7. In the following example, I use rootless voicings to play a one-chord **vamp** with a Latin feel.

To add more harmonic movement, you can turn this into a two-chord vamp by replacing G7 with Dm7–G7.

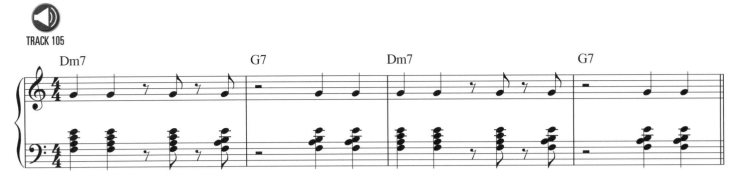

Any of the dominant 7th chords in the Diagram of Chord Subs can be expanded into a iim7–V7. To demonstrate this, let's start with a progression that makes use of secondary dominants and tritone subs.

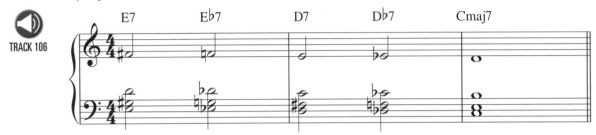

Here is the same progression with each dominant 7th chord expanded into a iim7–V7. Dizzy Gillespie used the progressions from Tracks 106 and 107 as reharmonizations of measures 3-4 of the jazz standard "I Can't Get Started."

When dominant 7th(♭9) chords are expanded into two chords, it is common to play ii∅7–V7♭9, generally referred to as a minor II–V. (See *JPM*, page 75, for more about the minor II–V–I.) Here I start with V7♭9–Imaj7.

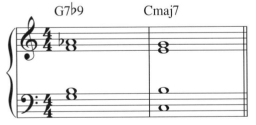

Here is how I could expand the progression from Track 108 to include ii∅7–V7♭9.

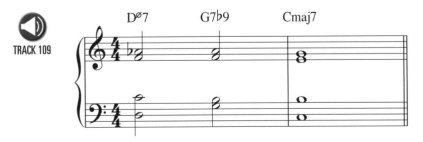

Practice: Look for opportunities to expand dominant 7th chords in tunes you play.

THE IV CHORD

Sometimes a progression includes both the Imaj7 and the iiim7.

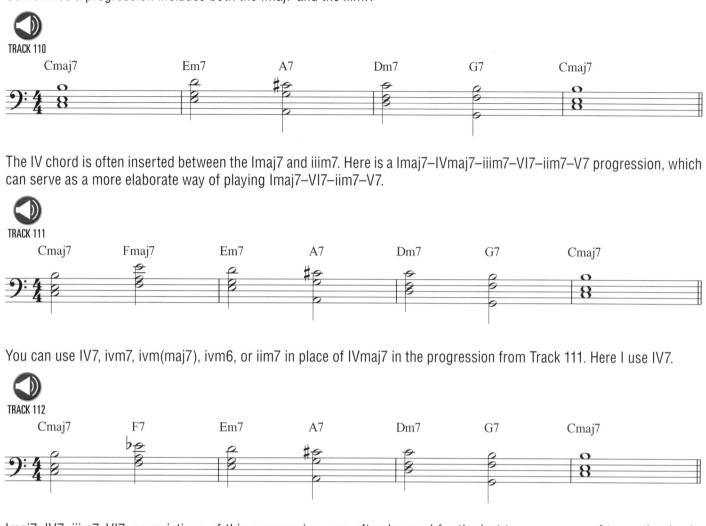

The IV chord is often inserted between the Imaj7 and iiim7. Here is a Imaj7–IVmaj7–iiim7–VI7–iim7–V7 progression, which can serve as a more elaborate way of playing Imaj7–VI7–iim7–V7.

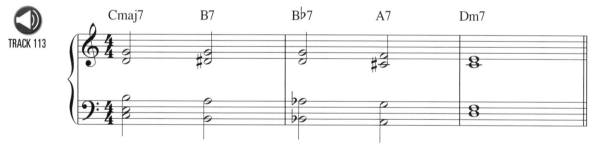

You can use IV7, ivm7, ivm(maj7), ivm6, or iim7 in place of IVmaj7 in the progression from Track 111. Here I use IV7.

Imaj7–IV7–iiim7–VI7, or variations of this progression, can often be used for the last two measures of tunes that begin on iim7 or II7, functioning as a turnaround back to the beginning of the form. Keep in mind that iiim7 can be replaced by III7. This allows for a common variation that replaces both III7 and IV7 with tritone subs. The result is a progression that descends chromatically from Imaj7 to VI7 and leads to iim7 or II7. Here is an example of this.

As you know, V7 often resolves to Imaj7 (or iiim7), but another way to lead to Imaj7 (or iiim7) is to use ivm7, ivm(maj7), or ivm6. In the following example, I use Fm7 (ivm7) as a way to lead to Cmaj7 (Imaj7).

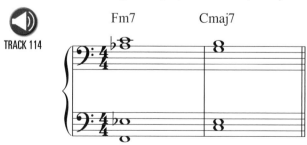

It's common to follow ivm7 with ♭VII7 before moving to Imaj7 (or iiim7) or to use ♭VII7 in place of ivm7. In the following example I use ivm7–♭VII7 (Fm7 – B♭7) to lead to Imaj7 (Cmaj7). Notice that ivm7–♭VII7 forms a iim7–V7 in another key.

Practice: Examine tunes you play and locate where the IV chord is used. Experiment to see where you can use the variations that were presented in this section.

THE TADD DAMERON TURNAROUND

Tadd Dameron, the great bebop composer, arranger, and pianist, wrote "Lady Bird," a 16-bar tune that has become a jazz standard. The last two measures contain a unique turnaround that has become known as "the Tadd Dameron turnaround." The progression is derived from Imaj7–VI7–II7–V7, but uses a tritone sub in place of VI7 that resolves to a major 7th chord that is a major 3rd lower than the original key. The V7 chord is also replaced by a tritone sub that leads back to Imaj7.

Here is the Tadd Dameron turnaround leading back to Imaj7.

Practice: Learn to play the Tadd Dameron turnaround in other keys. Try applying it to tunes as an interesting turnaround, or use it to create an intro or ending.

THE DIMINISHED 7th CHORD

In *JPM*, pages 79-82, you learned about the diminished scale. You also learned how diminished 7th chords are related to dominant 7th chords. For example, G7♭9 is related to B°7 because the 3rd, 5th, 7th, and ♭9th of G7♭9 form B°7. Sometimes a diminished 7th chord is used as a substitute for a dominant 7th(♭9) chord. Notice in the following example how C#°7 is used as a sub for A7, and then resolves up a half step to Dm7.

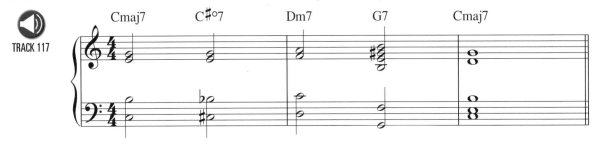

There are other instances in which a diminished 7th chord resolves up a half step to a minor 7th chord. In the next example, I use a diminished 7th chord to lead to iim7 (as in Track 117) and I also use a diminished 7th chord to lead up a half step to iiim7. This type of chord movement is the basis for the opening bars of tunes such as "It Could Happen to You," "Memories of You," "On a Slow Boat to China," and "Serpent's Tooth." Here I use this chord movement to lead to iiim7–VI7–II7–V7–Imaj7.

Here is one more example of a diminished 7th chord that leads up a half step to a minor 7th chord, this time to vim7. The opening measures of "My One and Only Love" can be played using this type of chord movement.

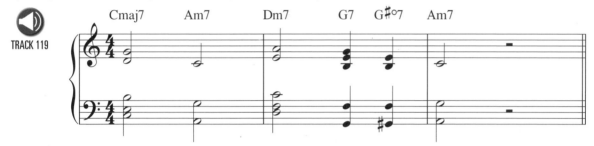

A diminished 7th chord can function as ♭iii°7 preceding iim7. The ♭iii°7 is sometimes used in place of vim7 in a Imaj7–vim7–iim7–V7 or iiim7–vim7–iim7–V7 progression. In the following example, I do the latter before resolving to Imaj7. The B section of "Someday My Prince Will Come" contains a good example of this type of movement.

Improvising tip: When improvising over a diminished 7th chord that leads up a half step to a minor chord or that functions as ♭iii°7 and precedes iim7, you can use a diminished scale, or you can use the Jewish scale that begins a major 3rd below. In the following example, I improvise over a repeated iiim7–♭iii°7–iim7–V7 in C. In measure 2, I use a diminished scale and in measure 6, I play down from the 7th of the B7 Jewish scale.

A chord progression similar to the one from Track 120 uses ♭iiim7 rather than ♭iii°7 in place of vim7 in a iiim7–vim7–iim7–V7 progression. The resulting progression, iiim7–♭iiim7–iim7–V7, is sometimes used for bars 3-4 of the A section of rhythm changes. (For more about rhythm changes, see *JPM*, pages 87-88.) Here is iiim7–♭iiim7–iim7–V7–Imaj7 in C.

A diminished 7th chord can also be used in place of Imaj7, and will often resolve back to the original Imaj7. This is effective when the melody note that coincides with Imaj7 is either a chord tone or an upper extension of i°7. For example, if the melody note over Imaj7 is its root, 9th, 6th (13th), or 7th, substituting a diminished 7th chord will work. Here's an example of i°7 resolving to Imaj7 in the context of a iim7–V7–Imaj7. The melody note at the start of the second bar was the 9th of Imaj7, so inserting i°7 worked well.

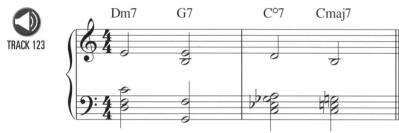

Sometimes we use a dominant 7th(♭9) chord or ii∅7–V7♭9 as a substitute for a diminished 7th chord. For example, in the key of B♭, C♯°7 can function as ♭iii°7 and lead to Cm7 (iim7). Jazz musicians sometimes substitute A7♭9 for the C♯°7 in this situation. A7♭9 is related to C♯°7 because its 3rd, 5th, 7th, and ♭9th form C♯°7. This can be taken one step further by expanding A7♭9 to be E∅7–A7♭9. Here's an example of this type of substitution. You may recognize this progression as the first four measures of "Stella by Starlight."

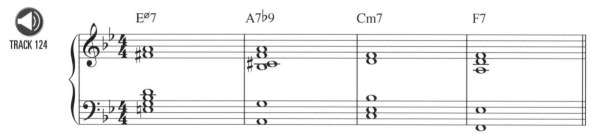

Practice: Learn to play these progressions that involve diminished 7th chords or subs for diminished 7th chords. Transpose them to other keys and practice improvising over them.

CHROMATIC APPROACH CHORDS

Track 103 showed how you can play dominant 7th chromatic approach chords. It is also possible to use a chromatic approach chord that is of the same chord quality as the one it approaches. For example, you might precede a minor 7th chord with another minor 7th chord from a half step above. Here is a progression in which I have included Fm7 as a chromatic approach chord that precedes Em7.

Another possibility is to precede a major 7th chord with another major 7th chord from a half step above. Here is a progression in which I have included D♭maj7 as a chromatic approach chord that precedes Cmaj7.

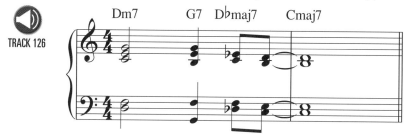

TRACK 126

A half-diminished chord is sometimes preceded by a minor 7th chord that is a half step above. To demonstrate this technique, let's start with a series of minor II–Vs that resolve to Imaj7. The last section of "Stella by Starlight" and the A section of Dizzy Gillespie's composition "Woody'n You" use a similar progression stretched over eight measures.

TRACK 127

Here I have added minor 7th chromatic approach chords that precede half-diminished chords.

TRACK 128

Voicing tip: If you can reach a 10th with your left hand, play the root of a closed-shell voicing an octave lower than usual to create a fuller sound. This is especially effective when playing solo piano. If you can't reach a 10th, try a quick "roll" (play the notes of the 10th in quick succession from low to high, as opposed to simultaneously). Here I apply this voicing technique to the example from Track 128.

TRACK 129

Practice: Experiment with tunes that you play to discover where you can include chromatic approach chords.

COLTRANE CHANGES

John Coltrane, the highly influential jazz saxophonist and composer, recorded his composition "Giant Steps" in 1959. The first half of the tune makes use of a harmonic progression that involves three major 7th chords that descend in major 3rds, each preceded by its V7.* This type of harmonic movement is sometimes referred to as the **Coltrane cycle** or **Coltrane changes**. Four different cycles can be created using this pattern. Here I play them using rootless voicings.

TRACK 130

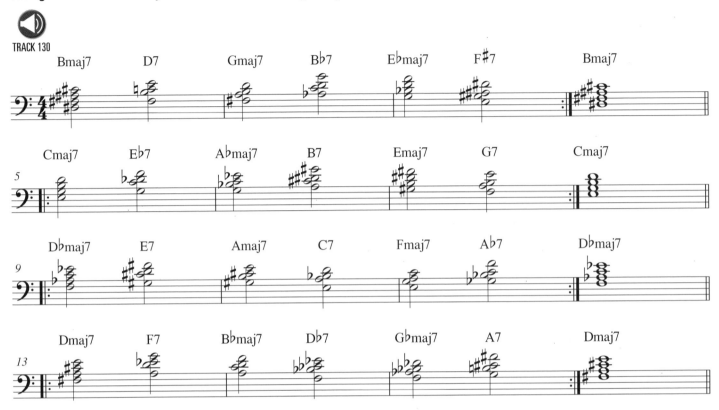

Trane used this pattern in a number of his compositions and reharmonizations of standards. Here's an example of how he applied it to a iim7–V7–Imaj7 in C. Notice that he begins on Dm7 (iim7) and then moves up a half step to a dominant 7th chord (Eb7) to begin the "Coltrane cycle." The progression moves through the keys of Ab and E before reaching the G7 (V7) that resolves back to Imaj7 (Cmaj7).

TRACK 131

Practice: Listen to John Coltrane play "Giant Steps" and "Countdown" and look at lead sheets to analyze the progressions of these tunes. Learn to play the four "Coltrane cycles" and the modified iim7–V7–Imaj7 in all keys, and practice improvising over them. This will prepare you to play Coltrane tunes and arrangements that use this harmonic progression.

*The second half of the tune "Giant Steps" involves major 7th chords that *ascend* in major 3rds, each preceded by its iim7–V7.

Chapter 4
JAZZ MELODIC MINOR SCALE THEORY

THE JAZZ MELODIC MINOR SCALE

In *JPM*, pages 76-77, you learned about the jazz melodic minor scale. This scale is like a major scale, but with a flatted third degree. It is played the same way up and down, unlike the classical version of the melodic minor scale that is played differently when descending. Here is the C jazz melodic minor scale, from now on referred to as simply the melodic minor scale.

TRACK 132

Jazz musicians typically use the melodic minor scale when improvising over minor-major 7th and minor 6th chords. For example, you could use the C melodic minor scale to improvise over Cm(maj7) or Cm6. Here's a line over Cm6.

TRACK 133

If you start on the first note of the melodic minor scale and play every other note as you ascend, a minor-major 7th chord with three extensions (9th, 11th, 13th) can be formed. Because every note in the melodic minor scale functions as either a chord tone or an upper extension, there are no weak tones. This means you don't have to be concerned with playing any of the notes as passing tones when you improvise with it; everything you play will work with the chord. Here is Cm(maj7), with the extensions 9th, 11th, 13th, that can be formed from the C melodic minor scale.

TRACK 134

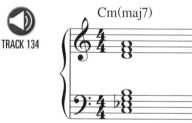

Practice: Play the jazz melodic minor scale in all keys and practice improvising with it over minor-major 7th and minor 6th chords.

THE LYDIAN DOMINANT SCALE

Like the modes of the major scale, the modes of the melodic minor scale are useful when improvising over various chord qualities. The fourth mode, the **Lydian dominant scale**, contains the same notes as a Mixolydian mode, but with the fourth note raised by a half step. This raised 4th can also be called the #11th. Here is the F Lydian dominant scale, which is the fourth mode of the C melodic minor scale. It is sometimes used to improvise over a dominant 7th chord.

TRACK 135

If you start on the first note of the Lydian dominant scale and play every other note as you ascend, a dominant 7th chord with three extensions (9th, #11th, 13th) can be formed. Every note in the Lydian dominant scale functions as either a chord tone or an upper extension of a dominant 7th chord, so there are no weak tones. Here is F7, with the extensions 9th, #11th, 13th, that can be formed from the F Lydian dominant scale.

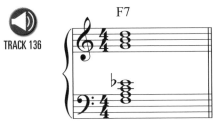

You may be wondering when to use the Lydian dominant scale. The short answer: You can use this scale over a dominant 7th chord upon which the 9th, #11th, and 13th sound appropriate. But when would that be? Most commonly, it's when a dominant 7th chord does not resolve down a 5th or up a 4th. For example, you would likely play a Lydian dominant scale when playing over IV7 or ♭VII7, preceding Imaj7 or iiim7. It is also frequently used when playing over a tritone sub. To feature the quirky sound of the #11th, it can be applied to the I7 of a blues or over the III7, VI7, II7, and V7 chords on the bridge of rhythm changes. Jazz musicians sometimes like to play the Lydian dominant scale on II7 preceding iim7, like on the second chord of Billy Strayhorn's "Take the A-Train."

To understand why the Lydian dominant scale is sometimes preferred over the Mixolydian mode, let's take a look at the progression below that involves Cmaj7 (Imaj7) and B♭7 (♭VII7). Prior to this discussion, you may have been inclined to simply use B♭ Mixolydian (or B♭ dominant bebop scale material) over the B♭7. The B♭ Mixolydian mode contains an E♭ that is outside of the key of C major and therefore has the potential to sound out of place in this context. Most experienced improvisers would opt to use the B♭ Lydian dominant scale over B♭7 here because the E♮ that is in the scale functions as the #11th of B♭7. E♮ is a note within the key of C major and therefore conveniently fits the harmonic context. In the following example, I improvise using the C major scale over Cmaj7 and the B♭ Lydian dominant scale over B♭7.

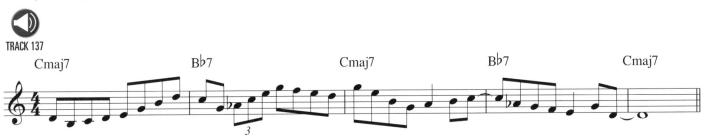

When you improvise over a chord progression that contains dominant 7th chords, you will have to make some decisions about which scales to use. You will have to determine whether the natural 4th of the Mixolydian or the raised 4th (#11th) of the Lydian dominant scale is the appropriate choice. Or you might find that a Jewish scale, altered scale, diminished scale, or whole tone scale works best. (See *JPM*, Chapter 9, for more about these scales.) Experiment with different options and use your ears to help you decide. To get a handle on some of these options and the decision-making process, let's consider the progression below, which contains several dominant 7th chords. These chords form the A section of Horace Silver's bossa nova-styled composition, "Song for My Father."

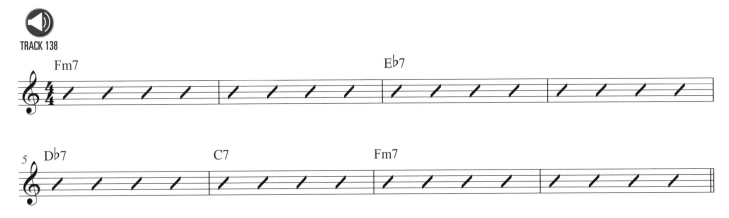

The progression in Track 138 centers around the key of F minor. This impacts which scales you might choose when improvising. Over the E♭7, I would most likely use the E♭ Mixolydian mode (or E♭7 bebop scale material) rather than the E♭ Lydian dominant scale. This is because the 4th of E♭ Mixolydian is A♭, a note that fits in well with the key center of F minor. Over the D♭7, however, I would likely use D♭ Lydian dominant rather than D♭ Mixolydian because the G♮ in the scale fits within the F minor tonality. The C7 is functioning as the V7 in a minor key, so it is typical to use the Jewish scale, altered scale, or diminished scale. Here is an example of an improvisation over the A section of "Song for My Father" using scales I've been discussing. I used the F blues scale over Fm7, E♭7 bebop scale material over E♭7, D♭ Lydian dominant scale over D♭7, and C7 Jewish scale material over C7.

TRACK 139

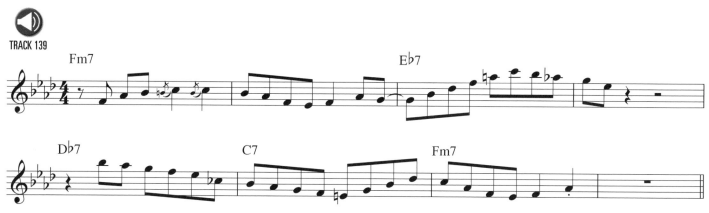

Practice: Play the Lydian dominant scale in all keys and practice improvising with it. Look for dominant 7th chords in tunes you play to find appropriate places to put it to use.

THE LOCRIAN ♯2 SCALE

The sixth mode of the melodic minor scale is called the **Locrian ♯2 scale**. It contains the same notes as the Locrian mode, but with the second note raised by a half step. (See *JPM*, page 34, for more about the Locrian mode.) Like the Locrian mode, it can be used when improvising over half-diminished chords. Here is the A Locrian ♯2 scale, which is the sixth mode of the C melodic minor scale. It can be used to improvise over A∅7.

TRACK 140

If you start on the first note of the Locrian ♯2 scale and play every other note as you ascend, a half-diminished 7th chord with three extensions (9th, 11th, ♭13th) can be formed. Because every note in the Locrian ♯2 scale functions as either a chord tone or an upper extension, there are no weak tones. Here is A∅7 with the extensions 9th, 11th, ♭13th that can be formed from the A Locrian ♯2 scale.

TRACK 141

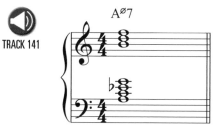

When using the Locrian mode over a half-diminished chord, the second note functions as the ♭9th. Because this note is neither a chord tone nor an extension, we can describe it as a weak tone. For this reason, it's typically used as a passing tone. The Locrian ♯2 scale, however, contains the natural 9th, an extension. Players of the 1940s and '50s usually opted for the Locrian mode (or the related dominant scale), but the Locrian ♯2 scale has become prevalent in more recent decades. (See *JPM*, page 76, for an explanation of how the Locrian mode relates to the Mixolydian mode and dominant bebop scale.) The harmonic context may also influence which scale you choose, so use your ears to help you decide which seems most appropriate.

In the following example, I improvise over iii∅7–VI7–ii∅7–V7–Imaj7. I used the E Locrian mode over E∅7, but over D∅7 I used the D Locrian ♯2 scale. This is simply one approach to this situation and you can experiment to decide which of these scales you want to use.

Practice: Play the Locrian ♯2 scale in all keys and practice improvising with it. Use this scale over half-diminished chords in tunes you play and compare the sound of it to the Locrian mode to decide which one you want to use in a given situation.

THE ALTERED SCALE

In *JPM*, pages 78-79, you learned about the altered scale, the seventh mode of the melodic minor scale. Here is the B7 altered scale, which is the seventh mode of the C melodic minor scale. The scale contains three basic chord tones of a dominant 7th (root, 3rd, 7th) and all of the altered dominant extensions (♭9th, ♯9th, ♯11th, ♭13th). (The 3rd of B7 is D♯, but for the notation, I used E♭, the enharmonic equivalent.) Because every note in the altered dominant scale functions as either a chord tone or an upper extension, there are no weak tones.

In the following example, I use the B7 altered scale over B7 before resolving to Em7.

Practice: Play the altered scale in all keys and review the exercises in *JPM*, pages 78-79, that show effective ways of using it in a progression.

RELATED SCALES AND RELATED CHORDS

So far, we have discussed the melodic minor scale and three of its modes. You have learned that the C melodic minor scale, the F Lydian dominant scale, the A Locrian ♯2 scale, and the B7 altered scale all share the same notes and none of these scales contain any weak tones. Therefore, when you improvise with these scales over chords, you may find it easier to simply think in terms of a melodic minor scale rather than the various modes.

For example, you can play a C melodic minor scale over F7♯11 rather than thinking of F Lydian dominant scale. Therefore, you can play a melodic minor scale that begins on the 5th of a dominant 7th(♯11) chord.

Similarly, you can play a C melodic minor scale over Aø7 rather than thinking of the A Locrian ♯2 scale. Therefore, play a melodic minor scale that begins on the 3rd of a half-diminished chord.

Over B7alt, you can play a C melodic minor scale instead of thinking of the B7 altered scale. Therefore, play a melodic minor scale that begins on the ♭9th of an altered dominant 7th chord.

The advantage of thinking in terms of melodic minor scales rather than modes is that it makes it easy to play the same melodic minor scale vocabulary over several different chord qualities. In the next example, I play the same C melodic minor scale phrase over Cm(maj7), Cm6, F7, Aø7, and B7alt.

Here is another way to understand how melodic minor scale-derived chords are related. In the following example, I play F7 with extensions (9th, ♯11th, 13th). I then move the root of this chord up two octaves to create an inversion that forms Aø7 with extensions (9th, 11th, ♭13th). Next, I move the root of Aø7 up two octaves to create an inversion that forms Cm(maj7) with extensions (9th, 11th, 13th). These three chords are related because, with extensions included, they are inversions of each other. Cm6 is also related to these chords because it is commonly substituted for Cm(maj7) and it too is formed from notes of the C melodic minor scale. Because F7♯11, Aø7, Cm(maj7), and Cm6 are essentially the same chord, the same voicings are sometimes used for all of them. We will look at this in more detail in Chapter 5.

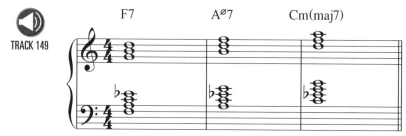

B7alt is also related to these chords because it is the tritone sub of F7. In the previous chapter, I explained that two dominant 7th chords a tritone apart are related because they share the same guide tones – the 3rd and 7th of one of the chords is the 7th and 3rd of the other. But that is just the basic relationship between these two dominant 7th chords. You will see that all the chord tones and extensions (including altered extensions) of a dominant 7th chord can also function as chord tones or extensions of a dominant 7th chord a tritone away. For example, C is the 5th of F7 but it is the ♭9th of B7. The diagram that follows shows how each note of the C melodic minor scale relates to F7 and B7. Use this information to help you understand these tritone relationships in all keys.

Diagram of Tritone Relationships

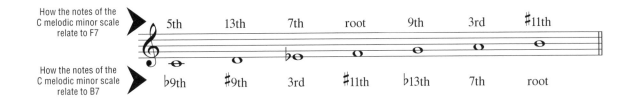

Understanding the relationships shown in the diagram above will help you when creating dominant voicings. Notice in the following example that the F7 rootless voicing is identical to the B7 altered rootless voicing. The roots are shown in parentheses because they are typically played by a bassist. (See *JPM*, page 64, for rootless voicing formulas.)

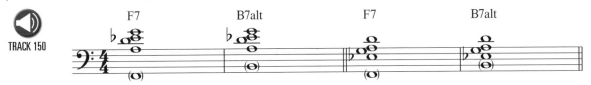

Practice: Play the exercise from Track 149 in all keys and review the relationship of dominant 7th chords that are a tritone apart. Use this information to help you understand how these chords are related to the melodic minor scale.

APPLYING THE MELODIC MINOR SCALE TO A CHORD PROGRESSION

Let's take a look at how we can use melodic minor scales to improvise over a chord progression. In the following example, I improvise over a minor II–V–I. Over D⌀7, I could use D Locrian (or B♭7 bebop scale material), but instead I use the F melodic minor scale. Remember that, instead of thinking of the D Locrian ♯2 scale, you can simply think of a melodic minor scale that begins on the 3rd of the half-diminished chord (as in Track 146). Over G7, I could play the Jewish scale or diminished scale, but here I use the A♭ melodic minor scale. Remember that, instead of thinking of the G7 altered scale, you can simply think of a melodic minor scale that begins on the ♭9th of an altered dominant 7th chord (as in Track 147). Over Cm6, I use the C melodic minor scale.

Practice: Use melodic minor scales to improvise over the minor II–V–I in all keys.

MELODIC MINOR SCALE VOCABULARY

In *JPM*, pages 76-77, I introduced the melodic minor scale and methods for improvising with it. You can use this material to improvise over any of the related chords that come from the melodic minor scale. Here are some more ideas that come from the C melodic minor scale that will help expand your vocabulary. These ideas can be played over Cm(maj7), Cm6, F7, A⌀7, and B7alt. Here I play them over Cm6.

TRACK 152

The ideas from Track 152 can be linked together or combined with melodic minor scale material from *JPM*. Here is an example that uses many of these ideas played over F7.

TRACK 153

When you play this material over an altered dominant 7th chord, you can also include the altered scale material such as the "Cry Me a River" lick or any of the four-note altered licks introduced in *JPM* (pages 78-79). Using these licks just before you resolve to a chord that is up a 4th or down a 5th can be particularly effective.

TRACK 154

Here's a useful ascending line that comes from the C melodic minor scale. It's a one-bar phrase that I repeated an octave higher. You can continue repeating the phrase to run up the whole keyboard.

TRACK 155

Cm(maj7), Cm6, F7, A⌀7, or B7alt

By starting at different points within this line, you can generate some useful one-bar melodic minor scale phrases that can be connected to other melodic minor scale ideas.

TRACK 156

Cm(maj7), Cm6, F7, A⌀7, or B7alt

This useful descending **run** comes from the C melodic minor scale. It uses a six-note phrase that can be repeated as you descend the keyboard.

TRACK 157

Cm(maj7), Cm6, F7, A⌀7, or B7alt

By starting at different points within the line used in Track 157, you can generate some useful one-bar phrases that can be applied to the chords derived from the melodic minor scale. In the following example, I show how these phrases can be played over B7alt and used to lead to Em7.

TRACK 158

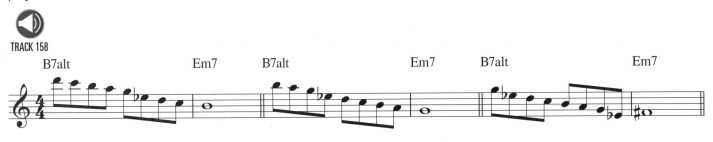

Practice: Learn to play melodic minor scale vocabulary in all keys. Practice connecting these ideas in different ways and apply this material to the related chords.

SOLO ON "BEAUTIFUL LOVE"

This solo on the chord progression of the standard "Beautiful Love" uses lots of the melodic minor scale vocabulary from this chapter, as well as from *JPM*. Analyze the solo to see which melodic minor scales are used.

TRACK 159

Practice: Learn to play this solo on "Beautiful Love" and improvise your own solos over this progression. Apply the melodic minor scale material from this chapter to other tunes in your repertoire.

Chapter 5
MOVABLE VOICINGS AND ACCOMPANIMENT STYLES

THE LOCKED-HANDS STYLE

Pianists occasionally play a chord below each note of a melody or improvised line. These chords that involve both hands playing the same rhythm are sometimes called **block chords**. They can be used for comping or to play a harmonized melodic line. There are different styles of block chords. In *JPM*, page 73, I showed you Red Garland's style of block chording. Milt Buckner developed another approach, made famous by George Shearing, called **locked-hands style**. This method requires both hands of the pianist to be joined together as if in handcuffs. The style typically involves playing a melody with the right hand, while the left hand doubles this melody in the octave below. Each note of the melody is harmonized with three notes played by the right hand. Here are the first eight measures of "Chicago (That Toddlin' Town)" played in locked-hands style.

TRACK 160

Notice that the three notes added below the melody in the right hand are mostly chord tones, but extensions may also be included. When the melody was moving quickly, I didn't play a chord with every note, but the illusion was created that each note was harmonized.

Practice: Learn to play this example of locked-hands style, and then apply this technique to other tunes.

MAJOR 6TH-DIMINISHED SCALE AND VOICINGS

It's important to remember that chords come from scales. We can achieve a more fluid approach to harmony by moving chords through scales. Barry Harris refers to a scale that contains the four notes of a major 6th chord and the four notes of a diminished 7th chord a half step below as a **major 6th-diminished scale**. Voicings can be created *from* this scale to move *through* this scale. Here is the C6-diminished scale, which you will recognize as being identical to a major bebop scale. As you can see, this scale is not a diminished scale, but rather derives its name from the fact that it contains the notes of a major 6th chord and the notes of a diminished 7th chord.

Using the notes of this scale, a four-note chord can be built up from each degree. A pattern results that alternates between C6 (and its inversions) and B°7 (and its inversions). Play up this series of chords and back down.

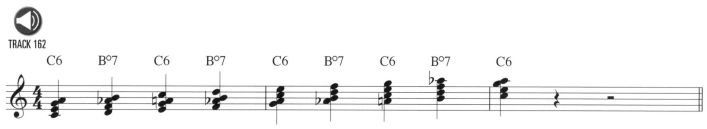

Since B°7 is related to G7♭9, it functions like a V7 that resolves back to the I chord (C6). So the series of chords C6–B°7–C6–B°7–C6–B°7–C6–B°7–C6 functions like I–V7–I–V7–I–V7–I–V7–I. The series of chords in Track 162 can be used for comping or to harmonize melodies over C6 or Cmaj7 and works best when the line moves **stepwise** so the alternating pattern can be included. The top note of the voicing will be heard as the melody and can be doubled an octave below by the left hand to create the locked-hands style. In Track 163, I applied these types of voicings to the opening of "Danny Boy." When the chord changed to C7, I switched to shell voicings. You can use the pedal, but be sure to clear the pedal with each and every chord.

Because C6 is an inversion of Am7, you can use the chords from Track 162 over Am7 for comping or to harmonize melodies. The B°7 from Track 162 is an inversion of G♯°7; G♯°7 is related to E7♭9, the V7 of Am7. So, the series of chords from Track 162 can function like Am7–E7♭9–Am7–E7♭9–Am7–E7♭9–Am7–E7♭9–Am7.

Here is the opening of "We Three Kings" using these voicings. The original chord for these four bars was A minor, but using the 6th-diminished scale generated chords with more harmonic motion.

In the following example, I harmonized the first eight bars of the old standard "Whispering" in locked-hands style. In the first two measures, where the original chord was B♭6, I harmonized the melody using chords from the B♭6-diminished scale, which created an alternating pattern of B♭6 and A°7. The original chord for measures 5-6 was Dm7, but I harmonized that section of the melody using the F6-diminished scale, which I used to create an alternating pattern of Dm7 and C♯°7. For the other measures, I used chord tones and some upper extensions to create other locked-hands voicings.

Practice: Learn to play the major 6th-diminished scale and the chords from Track 162 in all keys. Use these chords in locked-hands style to harmonize sections of melodies or as part of your comping.

MINOR 6TH-DIMINISHED SCALE AND VOICINGS

By flatting the third degree of the major 6th-diminished scale, a **minor 6th-diminished scale** can be formed that contains the four notes of a minor 6th chord and the four notes of a diminished 7th chord a half step below. You can also think of this scale as a jazz melodic minor scale with an added ♭6th. Here is the Cm6-diminished scale.

Using the notes of this scale, a four-note chord can be built up from each degree. A pattern results that alternates between Cm6 (and its inversions) and B°7 (and its inversions). Play up this series of chords and back down.

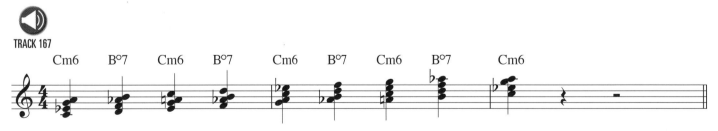

54

The series of chords in Track 167 can be used for comping or to harmonize melodies over Cm6 or Cm(maj7). In addition, they can be applied to related chords. Do you remember from Chapter 4 that Cm(maj7), Cm6, F7, A⌀7, and B7alt are all related? You can apply the series of chords from Track 167 to any of these related chords using the same scale-to-chord relationship concepts you learned about in Chapter 4. Specifically, that means you can form chords from the minor 6th-diminished scale that begins on the root of a minor 6th chord, the root of a minor-major 7th chord, the 3rd of a half-diminished chord, the 5th of a dominant 7th chord, or the ♭9th of an altered dominant 7th chord. In the following example, I formed chords over A⌀7 using the Cm6-diminished scale, used chords from the E♭m6-diminished scale over D7alt, and used chords from the Gm6-diminished scale over Gm6. I doubled the top note in the octave below to form locked-hands style voicings.

TRACK 168

Practice: Learn to play the minor 6th-diminished scale and the chords from Track 167 in all keys. Use these chords in locked-hands style to harmonize sections of melodies or as part of your comping.

DROP-TWO VOICINGS

A four-note chord that is voiced within the span of an octave can be referred to as a **four-note closed position voicing**. A **drop-two voicing** can be created from a four-note closed position voicing by shifting the second note from the top down an octave. Drop-two voicings are **open voicings**, voicings that span more than an octave, and can be used as a variation of the locked-hands style or can be used in combination with other voicing techniques. Here are drop-two voicings formed from the C6-diminished scale that can be used for C6, Cmaj7, or Amin7. Play up this series of chords and back down.

TRACK 169

Here are drop-two voicings formed from the Cm6-diminished scale that can be used for Cm6 or the related chords Cm(maj7), F7, A⌀7, and B7alt.

TRACK 170

Drop-two voicings can be formed from a diminished 7th chord and its inversions. Here is C♯°7 and its inversions. Use these chords over C♯°7, E°7, G°7, B♭°7, or over any of the related dominants (A7♭9, C7♭9, E♭7♭9, G♭7♭9).

TRACK 171

You can create a variation of the diminished drop-two voicings from Track 171 by using an upper extension of the diminished chord in place of one of the chord tones. (See *JPM*, page 59, for more about upper extensions of diminished 7th chords.) Use these chords over C#°7, E°7, G°7, B♭°7, or over any of the related dominants (A7♭9, C7♭9, E♭7♭9, G♭7♭9).

Here are drop-two voicings applied to a couple of common progressions.

Drop-two voicings can also be created from the major scale. Here is a way to play up a series of chords that comes from the C major scale. Notice that four of the chords are drop-two voicings that come from second-inversion chords; four of the chords are drop-two voicings that come from root-position chords. Play up this series of chords and back down.

Rather than alternating with diminished 7th chords as we did when using the 6th-diminished scale, the series of chords in Track 174 alternates between chords that relate to Cmaj7 and chords that relate to Dm7. When you use these chords to harmonize melodies or comp over Cmaj7 (Imaj7), the chords that suggest Dm7 (iim7) can be used as passing chords. When you harmonize melodies or comp over Dm7 (iim7), the chords that suggest Cmaj7 (Imaj7) can be used as passing chords.

Here are the chords from Track 174 that relate to Cmaj7.

Here are the chords from Track 174 that relate to Dm7.

TRACK 176

Here's another practice pattern to help you get used to playing these diatonic drop-two voicings.

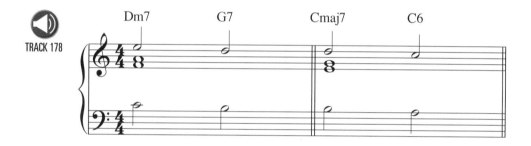

TRACK 177

Here's a common way to play iim7–V7–Imaj7 using drop two-voicings.

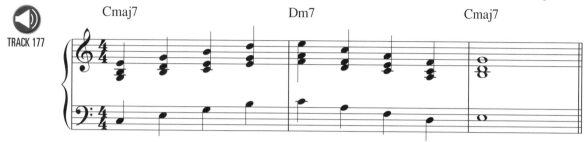

TRACK 178

Here's a more expanded way to play iim7–V7–Imaj7 using drop two-voicings. Notice that I used a couple of chords that come from the major 6th-diminished scale at the end of the progression.

TRACK 179

To demonstrate many of these voicing concepts, I've been playing simple rhythms. Try adding syncopation to make these progressions swing. Here is the series of chords from Track 179 played with more interesting rhythms.

TRACK 180

In Chapter 3, you learned about the tritone sub and you also learned how a dominant 7th chord (V7) can be expanded into two chords (iim7–V7). In the key of C, the tritone sub for G7 (V7) is Db7. If you expand the Db7 into two chords, you get Abm7–Db7, which can be used in place of Dm7–G7 to lead to Cmaj7. When you're comping, you can use drop-two voicings to play these chord subs, as in the following example.

TRACK 181

In this example, I play a iim7–V7 in C, followed by a iim7–V7 that is a tritone away, before resolving to Cmaj7. This makes an interesting variation on the conventional iim7–V7–Imaj7.

TRACK 182

Here are a couple more useful drop-two voicings that can be played for V7–Imaj7 or V7–I6.

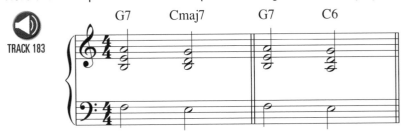

TRACK 183

The 9th and 13th of G7 in the previous example can be altered. In the following example, I resolve to C6, but I could have chosen to resolve to Cmaj7.

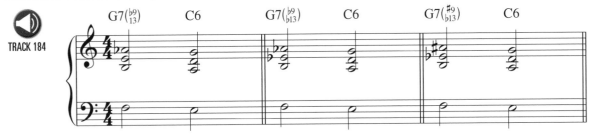

TRACK 184

The following example makes use of many of the drop-two techniques from this chapter.

TRACK 185

Practice: Learn to play drop-two voicings in all keys. Use these chords to harmonize sections of melodies and as part of your comping.

STRIDE

Stride is a piano style characterized by a left-hand technique that places a bass note on the first and third beats of each measure, and a middle register chord on the second and fourth beats. The "Father of Stride," James P. Johnson, helped develop what became the predominant jazz piano style of the 1920s and '30s. Other notable stride pianists included Willie "The Lion" Smith, Fats Waller, and Art Tatum.

The bass notes played on beats one and three are typically roots, but if a chord in a progression lasts for four beats or more, the bass notes may alternate between the root and 5th. An octave can be used in place of a single bass note, or a 10th or a 10th filled in with another note such as a 5th can be played by those with big hands. The middle register chords on beats two and four are often simply triads or four-note chords played in root position or inverted. You can also use rootless voicings, or even just the 3rd and 7th, or the 7th and 3rd of the chord. Here's an example of left-hand stride with a right-hand improvisation. If you can't reach a 10th, try a quick roll.

The great stride pianists were virtuosos who used many techniques in addition to the basic style described above. One of these techniques, **walking 10ths**, involves playing ascending or descending quarter-note lines in 10ths with the left hand, as in the first measure of the following example.

Here's the old standard "You Made Me Love You" played in a stride style.

Practice: Learn to play this stride version of "You Made Me Love You" and apply this style to other tunes in your repertoire.

WALKING BASS LINES

The bassist in a jazz group is largely responsible for providing the rhythmic and harmonic foundation of the music. When playing a swing feel, this can be achieved by playing a **walking bass line**, a continuous series of low-register quarter notes, with occasional rhythmic embellishments, composed of roots and other notes related to the harmony of the tune. In situations without a bassist, you may want to assume this role by playing bass lines with your left hand.

Walking bass lines can be formed from chord tones and scales, and can make use of passing tones. Often the connection from one chord to the next involves a half step or whole step to ensure a flowing line. Listen to great bassists like Ray Brown, Paul Chambers, and Ron Carter to hear how beautiful and creative bass lines can be.

To get started, let's create a walking line of quarter notes to accompany dominant 7th chords that last for two beats each and move through the cycle. Use your left hand to play the root of a dominant 7th chord and precede the root of each subsequent chord with a note that approaches from a half step above or below. This will create a strong pull into each new chord. With the right hand, you can add rootless voicings or simply play the 3rd and 7th, or the 7th and 3rd of each chord. The following example involves a cycle of dominant 7th chords, but you can apply this bass line technique to other chord qualities as well. I play voicings with the right hand that anticipate each chord change by an eighth note.

🔊
TRACK 189

Another option, when moving through the cycle, is to use the 3rd or 5th of a chord to connect to the root of the next chord. You will approach each chord from either a half step above or below, or from a whole step above or below. Here's a bass line for a cycle of iim7–V7s. With the right hand, I play voicings that anticipate each chord change by an eighth note.

TRACK 190

Chord tones can be used to form bass lines for chords that last for a full measure or more. Play the root at the start of each chord and use chord tones to complete the measure. The 7th of a chord can be used, but solid bass lines can often be formed by simply using the root, 3rd, and 5th. In the following example, I play a bass line for a cycle of dominant 7th chords that last for one measure each. For some of the chords, I use only chord tones, with the occasional inclusion of the 6th for variety, but for others I used a chromatic passing tone to connect to the root of the next chord. Notice how using the notes of an inverted triad is a good way to change the shape of the line and to keep the line from getting into a register that's too high.

TRACK 191

Many bass lines are **scalar**. The following example shows ways to play bass lines that involve scales with some added passing tones. The lowest E on the piano is the same pitch as the lowest string on a standard upright bass, so you can play the following exercise an octave lower than notated to sound even more bass-like.

For long durations of a chord, imply the V7 chord in spots to add harmonic interest and direction to the line. In the following example of a bass line for Cm7, I insert notes of G7 (the V7 of Cm7).

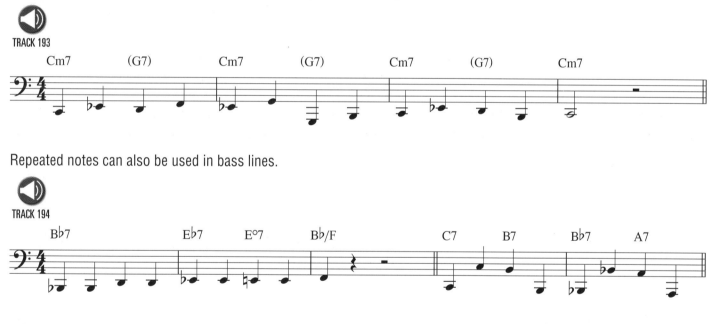

Repeated notes can also be used in bass lines.

Great bassists have many ways of rhythmically embellishing a line. One way is to play two swing-eighth notes in place of a quarter note in a bass line. This can involve repeating the same note or changing to another chord tone.

Another way to add rhythmic interest and syncopation is to anticipate a note by an eighth note.

Here's a bass line for "Autumn Leaves" that includes many of the techniques we've covered.

TRACK 197

8vb throughout

Practice: Get comfortable with these bass-line exercises. Use these techniques to create bass lines for tunes in your repertoire. Add chords with your right hand. You can also work on improvising lines with your right hand while you walk bass lines with your left.

LATIN STYLES

The musical traditions of Latin America have had an enormous impact on jazz music. When a jazz piece calls for a Latin feel, this could mean any number of different styles. It's a vast area of study, so here we'll take a look at just a few techniques as an introduction.

The term **Afro-Caribbean music** is used as an umbrella term to include various African-influenced musical styles of the Caribbean. Afro-Cuban and Puerto Rican styles were the foundation of the popular dance music developed in New York City in the 1960s that became known as **salsa**. Typically, all the musicians in a salsa group play rhythms that "fit" with a repeated two-bar rhythm known as the **clave**. (Types include son clave and rumba clave.)

Here's 3-2 son clave. The rhythmic pattern is played as written rather than swung.

TRACK 198

Here is 2-3 son clave.

TRACK 199

The pianist in a salsa group often plays a repeated figure known as a **montuno** or a **guajeo.** Here is a montuno in 2-3 clave that harmonizes iim7–V7–Imaj7–Imaj6.

TRACK 200

Samba and bossa nova music come from Brazil. Pianists comping in these styles sometimes play patterns that vary as the tune progresses. Here are some typical bossa nova comping rhythms.

TRACK 201

Practice: Learn to play these Latin accompaniment patterns in other keys and apply them to Latin tunes in your repertoire.

Chapter 6
MODERN SOUNDS

Much of what I have presented so far has focused on techniques and styles that were developed in the first half of the 20th century. This chapter will go into some of the trends that followed. McCoy Tyner, Herbie Hancock, and Chick Corea are three notable jazz pianists who came to prominence in the 1960s. Building upon the innovations of earlier artists, they developed and explored many of the "modern sounds" presented here and influenced the direction of jazz harmony and improvisation.

THE DOMINANT 7th(sus4) CHORD

In *JPM*, page 18, you learned about the dominant 7th(sus4) chord. "Sus4" is short for "suspended 4th," which means that the 3rd has been replaced with the 4th. Triads can also be suspended. Gsus4 is a G triad with the 3rd (B) replaced by the 4th (C) and Gsus2, also called simply G2, is a G triad with the 3rd (B) replaced by the 2nd (A). Here is a G7 suspended 4th chord. Symbols that can be used for this chord include G7sus4, G7sus, or G11.

If you add the 9th to G7sus, you will find that you have formed Dm7 over G. For this reason, the chord symbol "Dm7/G" is sometimes used in place of the symbol "G7sus." (In *JPM*, page 25, you learned that chord symbols with a slash are known as "slash chords." With this type of notation, the chord is indicated to the left of or above the slash, and the note required as the lowest is shown to the right of or below the slash.) You can think of a dominant 7th(sus4) chord as a iim7 with the root of the V7 in the bass. Here is Dm7/G.

To form voicings for G7sus when working in a group, you can simply use Dm7 voicings of any type and let the bassist supply the root, G. In a solo setting, either play G7 shell voicings with the 4th in place of the 3rd, or add a G in the bass register below any type of Dm7 voicing. The extensions of Dm7 (9th, 11th, 13th) are all appropriate when used in the G7sus context. When improvising over G7sus, play melodic material that is suitable over Dm7 (functioning as iim7). You might, for example, choose to use the D Dorian mode or the G7 bebop scale and related material. Here is an improvisation over G7sus using the D Dorian mode.

G7sus often precedes G7 before resolving to another chord. Here are some examples of that. Notice that I have added the 9th to G7sus and the ♭9th to the G7, which harmonize nicely with the 4th of the sus chord and the 3rd of G7, respectively.

TRACK 205

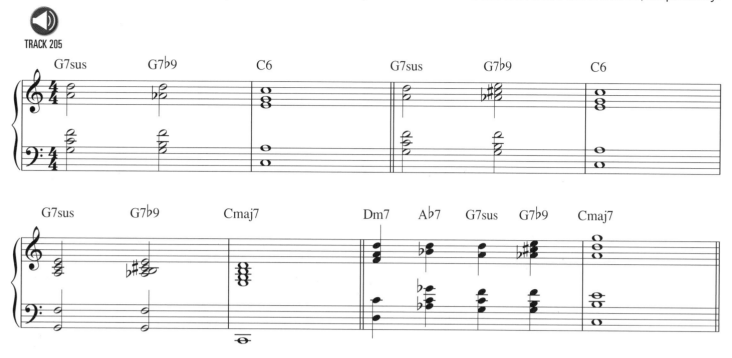

Jazz pianists and composers sometimes use dominant 7th(sus4) chords that *don't* resolve to an (unsuspended) dominant 7th chord as they did in Track 205. Bill Evans's recording "Peace Piece" (1958) is an early example of this. The tune is based on a progression that alternates between G7sus and Cmaj7 without ever including G7. The opening of "Flamenco Sketches" from Miles Davis's album *Kind of Blue* (1959) also includes this progression. In the following example, I apply this technique to the chord progression of the A section of "Afternoon in Paris" (see *JPM*, page 57-58). I replace each iim7–V7 with V7sus to create a progression that sounds a bit more modern than the original. On the following track, I use minor 7th rootless voicings in measures 2, 4, 6, and 8, and the bassist supplies the root of each sus chord. Remember that F7sus can be played as Cm7/F, E♭7sus can be played as B♭m7/E♭, and G7sus can be played as Dm7/G.

TRACK 206

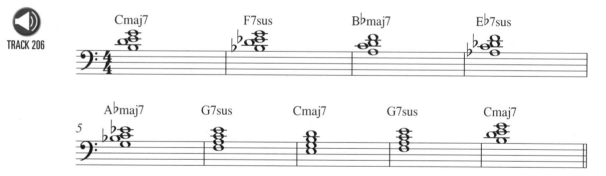

Herbie Hancock's composition "Maiden Voyage" (1965) is a piece that makes use of four-measure durations of dominant 7th(sus4) chords and is a classic example of **modal jazz**. Modal compositions use modes as the basis for chords, melodies, and improvisations. Typically, these pieces include long stretches based on a particular mode. Chords in modal tunes often move in nontraditional ways.

Practice: Learn to play dominant 7th(sus4) chords in all keys and practice improvising over them. Find places to use this type of chord as a sub for a V7 or iim7–V7.

THE DOMINANT 7th sus(♭9) CHORD

The dominant 7th sus(♭9) chord is another important modern sound. It's a dominant 7th(sus4) with the ♭9th added. Whereas G7sus can be described as Dm7/G, G7sus(♭9) can be described as D∅7/G. The John Coltrane Quartet, with McCoy Tyner on piano, used this type of chord extensively. Trane's modal composition "Africa" is based on just one chord, E7sus(♭9). Here is G7sus(♭9).

When improvising over G7sus(♭9), play melodic material that is appropriate over D∅7. You might, for example, choose to use the D Locrian mode or use the B♭7 bebop scale and related material. (See *JPM*, page 76, for an explanation of how to use a dominant bebop scale over a half-diminished chord.) When playing over G7sus(♭9), some musicians choose to think of the notes of the D Locrian mode (seventh mode of the E♭ major scale) as the G Phrygian mode (third mode of the E♭ major scale) because these two modes contain the same notes. For this reason, the dominant 7th sus(♭9) chord is sometimes referred to as a Phrygian chord. Here is an improvisation over G7sus(♭9) using the D Locrian mode (G Phrygian mode).

In Chapter 4, you learned that another way to improvise over a half-diminished chord is to use a jazz melodic minor scale. You can use the F jazz melodic minor scale to play over D∅7, so you can also use it over G7sus(♭9). In addition to the symbols G7sus(♭9) and D∅7/G, you can use Fm6/G, because D∅7 and Fm6 contain the same notes. Here's an improvisation over G7sus(♭9) using the F jazz melodic minor scale.

There are many ways to form voicings for G7sus(♭9). When working in a group, you can use D∅7 voicings and let the bassist supply the root, G. Any of the extensions of D∅7 (9th, 11th, ♭13th) can be used in the G7sus(♭9) context when comping for a solo or melody based on the F melodic minor scale. But when comping for a solo or melody based on the D Locrian mode (G Phrygian mode) or B♭7 bebop scale material, avoid voicings that include E (the 9th of D∅7). Another useful left-hand voicing to use in a group context can be formed by playing 1-♭9-4-5 of G. You can also use B♭7 unaltered rootless voicings, which (you should note) are inversions of the 1-♭9-4-5 voicing. When you want to include the root (in a solo setting, for example), use this 1-♭9-4-5 voicing, or play G7 shell voicings with the 4th in place of the 3rd, or add a G in the bass register below any type of D∅7 voicing.

In the following example, I use G7sus(♭9) as a sub for G7 in a iim7–V7–Imaj7 progression. I used the 1-♭9-4-5 voicing for G7sus(♭9) and improvised over it using the F jazz melodic minor scale.

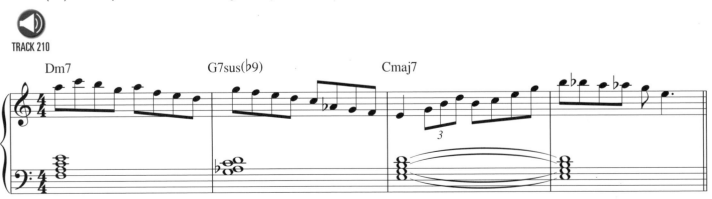

Practice: Learn to play dominant 7th sus(♭9) chords in all keys and practice improvising over them. Try using this type of chord as a sub for V7 in a iim7–V7–Imaj7 progression.

QUARTAL HARMONY

Our study of harmony thus far has focused on chords that are formed by stacking 3rds, or what is known as **tertian harmony**. The diatonic chords in *JPM*, pages 22-23, show how a scale can be used as the source for forming chords built in 3rds. Beginning in the 1960s, McCoy Tyner became known for his use of chords formed by stacking 4ths, or what is known as **quartal harmony**. In the example below, I formed three-note **4th voicings** from the D Dorian mode that can be used over stretches of Dm7. Notice that most of the intervals are perfect 4ths, but the third and seventh chords in the series contain an augmented 4th.

McCoy Tyner used chords from Track 211 as left-hand comping voicings when he improvised on modal tunes such as John Coltrane's "Impressions," which involves long stretches of D Dorian (Dm7). "Impressions" uses the same chord progression as "So What," a 32-measure tune with an AABA form that is based on just two modes. The A sections are based on D Dorian (Dm7) and the B section (the bridge) is based on E♭ Dorian (E♭m7). Playing a single minor 7th chord over and over would be monotonous, so McCoy was able to create harmonic interest by moving around with these 4th voicings.

When improvising on "Impressions," you can use the Dorian mode to create melodic lines and patterns, or you can use the dominant bebop scale and related material. For example, when improvising over the A sections, use the D Dorian mode or the G7 bebop scale and related material. To play over the bridge, use the E♭ Dorian mode or the A♭7 bebop scale and related material, and form 4th voicings from the E♭ Dorian mode.

In the following example, I improvise over the first eight bars of "Impressions" and use 4th voicings for my left-hand comping. In the right hand, I solo using the D Dorian mode.

To comp behind a soloist, the right hand can be used to stack more 4ths. Here's an example of four- and five-note 4th voicings that can be formed from the D Dorian mode, which can be used to comp over stretches of Dm7.

TRACK 213

The fifth and sixth chords in the five-note voicings from Track 213 can be inverted by moving the lowest note to the top to form two voicings that are sometimes called "So What" chords – because Bill Evans played these voicings on the original recording of that tune. Play the higher voicing followed by the lower voicing from the example below and you will hear the sound of this classic tune. Here are the "So What" chords that come from the D Dorian mode. They can be used when comping over D Dorian (Dm7). Notice that these voicings are identical, but a whole step apart.

TRACK 214

Here's a chordal pattern using the "So What" chords that could be used for an introduction or comping pattern for a modal tune like "Impressions." At the start of the pattern, I play the root and 5th of Dm7 in the bass register. This is a signature McCoy sound that that can be used to mark the start of sections in a tune. In the example, I demonstrate how this can be played on beat one, on the "and of 4," or on beat four.

TRACK 215

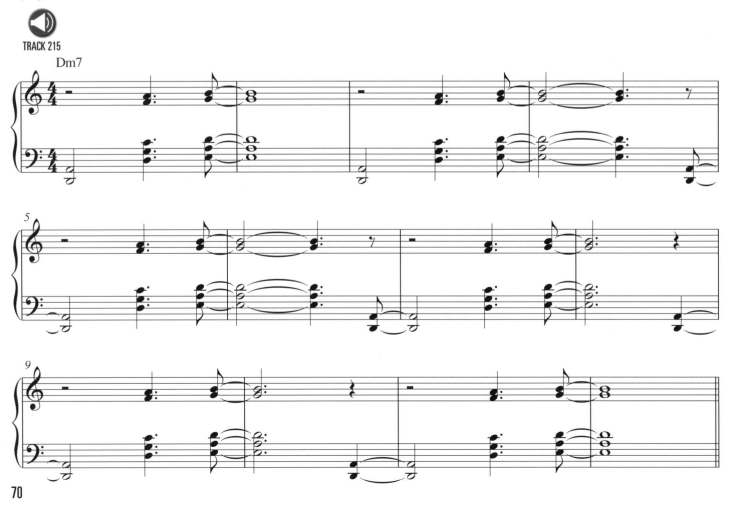

McCoy often played a series of chords that included the two "So What" chords along with the third, fifth, and sixth of the five-note voicings from Track 213. Here is the five-chord series that can be used to play over D Dorian (Dm7). This pattern can be repeated in higher octaves, forming a series of chords that can be played up and down the piano.

The 4th voicings presented in Tracks 211, 213, 214, and 216 can also be applied to a dominant 7th chord. To do this, think of a dominant 7th chord as V7 and apply the 4th voicings that relate to iim7. For example, to play over G7(V7), play the 4th voicings that come from D Dorian and relate to Dm7(iim7). Some of the voicings contain the 4th of G7, so G7sus (V7sus) will be implied. This only helps to further enhance the modern sound. In the following example, I comp over a G blues progression using the five-chord series of 4th voicings presented in Track 216. In the fourth measure, I used D♭7, a tritone sub for G7, so I played 4th voicings that relate to A♭m7 (A♭ Dorian). For the measures of C7, I used 4th voicings that relate to Gm7 (G Dorian), and for the measure of D7, I used 4th voicings that relate to Am7 (A Dorian). The first chord of the example introduces another useful voicing for a dominant 7th. It's formed by adding one more note a 4th above the third five-note voicing in Track 213, creating a six-note 4th voicing. (Whew!)

Some of the 4th voicings from Track 213 and 214 can also be applied to Cmaj7 or C6. For example, the second five-note voicing in Track 213 can be used as a voicing for C6. This chord can be inverted by moving the lowest note to the top to form a "So What" chord that also works for C6. The sixth five-note voicing in Track 213 can be used as a voicing for Cmaj7, as can its inversion, a "So What" chord that was presented in Track 214. When playing in a group, the bassist can supply the root of the major chord, but in a solo setting you can add the root below these voicings.

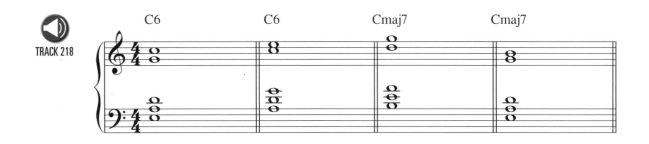

In the next example, I comp over Cmaj7 and use some of these voicings. In measure 5, I move the "So What" chord down a whole step and then back up, and in measure 7, I move it up and down chromatically to create harmonic movement.

Practice: Learn to play 4th voicings and "So What" chords in all keys. Include them in your comping on tunes with long stretches of a single chord.

MODAL PATTERNS AND LINES

The long stretches of a single chord in modal tunes are conducive to playing melodic patterns that move through a scale. Here are examples of some diatonic patterns that ascend and descend. In these examples, I'm playing over Dm7 and the lines are based on the D Dorian mode. These same patterns, or others that you invent, can be applied to other modes.

Now we'll examine melodic vocabulary that McCoy Tyner used for some of his modal playing in the 1960s. He often played four-note ideas derived from the Dorian mode. These ideas sometimes included the 6th rather than the 7th of the Dorian mode, or involved the 7th resolving to the 6th. Here are some ascending ideas derived from the D Dorian mode. Each can be repeated in higher octaves to create a run up the keyboard, or you can alternate between different ideas to create a run. A variation of the idea in the first measure can be created by moving the first note up a whole step to E.

The next example shows some descending ideas derived from the D Dorian mode. Notice that some of these ideas are the same as the ascending ones from Track 221 played backward. **Retrograde** is the musical term for a series of notes played backward. These four-note ideas can be connected in various sequences to create longer lines.

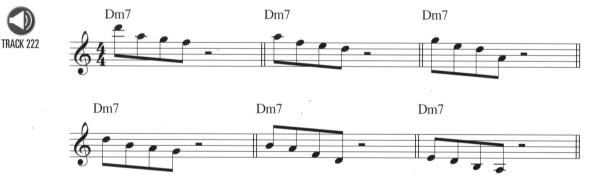

The following idea can be used to change the direction of a line from descending to ascending. The first measure shows the basic idea and measures 2-3 show it in context.

Here is an idea that can be used to change the direction of a line from ascending to descending. The first measure shows the basic idea and measures 2-3 show it in context.

Here are a couple of ideas for the ends of phrases.

The improvisation over Dm7 in Track 226 makes use of all the ideas from Tracks 221-225. These melodic ideas can also be used over other related chords within the key. Here, I play them over Dm7, but they can also be used over other chords that come from the key of C: G7, G7sus, B⌀7, and E7sus(♭9). They can also be played over Fmaj7♯11. (There's more about major 7th(♯11) chords later in this chapter.) With the left hand, try comping with 4th voicings.

TRACK 226

Practice: Learn to play the modal patterns and lines in this section in all keys. Practice connecting ideas in different ways and apply this material to tunes in your repertoire.

PENTATONIC SCALES

In Chapter 2, you learned about the major and minor pentatonic scales. These five-note scales lack half steps and don't allow you to create certain intervals (e.g., minor 2nds, tritones, and major 7ths). This somewhat limited palette may seem like a negative quality, but when you start experimenting with them, you'll discover this makes it easy to form pleasing melodies. These scales can be useful when improvising on a number of different chord qualities. We've discussed using the Dorian mode when improvising over a minor 7th chord. Leaving out the 2nd and 6th degrees of the Dorian mode will leave you with the notes of a minor pentatonic scale.

Here's an example of an improvisation over Dm7 using the D minor pentatonic scale.

Another possibility is to use the minor pentatonic scale that begins on the 9th of a minor 7th chord. This creates a colorful sound because the extensions of the minor 7th chord (9th, 11th, 13th) are all contained within the scale. In the following example, I use the F minor pentatonic scale to improvise over the bridge of "Impressions," eight measures of E♭m7. With your left hand, you can play three-note 4th voicings based on E♭ Dorian.

You can improvise over a dominant 7th chord or over a dominant 7th(sus4) chord with a major pentatonic scale that begins on the root of the chord. In the following example, I improvise over F7sus using the F major pentatonic scale (equivalent to the D minor pentatonic scale). With your left hand, you can play three-note 4th voicings that come from the C Dorian mode.

To play over an altered dominant 7th chord, use a major pentatonic scale that begins on the #11th of the chord. The result is a pentatonic scale that contains all four altered dominant extensions (♭9th, #9th, #11th, ♭13th). In the following example, I used the E♭ major pentatonic scale (equivalent to the C minor pentatonic scale) over A7alt.

There are a few ways to use a major pentatonic scale over a major chord. The most straightforward approach is to use the major pentatonic scale that begins on the root of the chord. Another option is to use the major pentatonic scale that begins on the 5th of a major chord. If you want to include the #11th, use a major pentatonic scale that begins on the 9th of a major chord. This last use of the scale is related to the Lydian mode, which we will discuss later in this chapter. Use these scales to improvise lines. Or play a scale up the piano with the sustain pedal pressed down to create a run over the final major chord of a tune, as in the following examples. Over C6, I played the C major pentatonic scale; over Cmaj7, I played the G major pentatonic scale and the D major pentatonic scale.

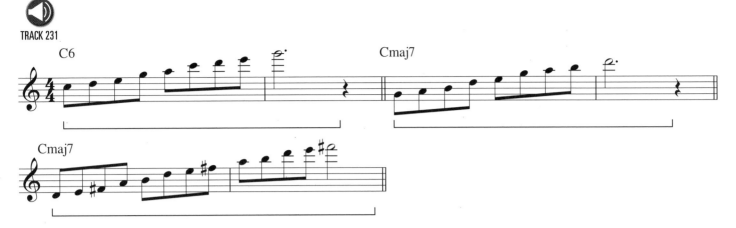

TRACK 231

Practice: Learn to play major and minor pentatonic scales in all keys. Apply them to different chords as described in this section.

PLAYING "OUTSIDE"

Most jazz musicians have played outdoor gigs and have had to deal with rain, bugs, and all sorts of adverse conditions. This section of the book, however, has nothing to do with this! When jazz musicians talk about playing "outside," they are talking about improvising in a way that is outside the norms of traditional harmony. Using a chord substitution such as a tritone sub as the basis for a melodic line, for example, can create a departure from the expected harmony. In this line over a iim7–V7–Imaj7 in C, I played a phrase over G7 that comes from D♭7 Mixolydian. The phrase I used includes the 4th of D♭7, which sounds "out" when played over G7.

TRACK 232

Playing "out" can be particularly effective when playing a modal tune or modal section of a tune. A long stretch of a single chord lacks the tension and release we find in the harmony of most jazz standards. Playing "out" and then coming back "inside" can create the effect of tension and release. When playing "out," the keys you move into can be arbitrary or follow a pattern. Extremely "outside" playing may even be **atonal** (without a tonal center).

Right Hand "In" and Left Hand "Out"

In the following example, I solo over two A sections of "Impressions." In the first four bars, I improvise with the D minor pentatonic scale in my right hand. In my left hand, I begin comping with 4th voicings from the D Dorian mode, but starting in measure 3, I go "out" by using 4th voicings from the E♭ Dorian mode before moving back to a 4th voicing from D Dorian at the end of measure 4 to come back "in." Hearing these two tonalities at the same time creates tension. The use of two keys at the same time is called **bitonality**, and it's a common way to create an "outside" effect.

Right Hand "Out" and Left Hand "In"

In measures 5-8, I keep my left-hand comping "inside" by sticking with harmonies formed from the D Dorian mode. My right-hand solo uses vocabulary that comes from D Dorian until measure 7, when I start going "out" by improvising with the F minor pentatonic scale. F minor pentatonic contains three notes (A♭, B♭, and E♭) that clash with the D Dorian mode. This bitonal sound creates tension that then resolves toward the end of measure 8.

Both Hands "Out"

In measures 9-12, both the solo line and the comping depart from the original tonality. I play harmonies and a melodic line that come from a series of Dorian modes based on a diminished scale pattern (D Dorian, E Dorian, F Dorian, G Dorian, A♭ Dorian, B♭ Dorian, B Dorian, C♯ Dorian) before coming back "inside" by returning to four measures based on D Dorian.

TRACK 233

Practice: Experiment with playing "outside." Start with a modal tune like "Impressions" and practice going "out" with your right hand while your left hand stays "in." Then try just the opposite; keep your right hand "in" while your left hand goes "out." You can also try going "out" with both hands. Use these techniques to set up tension and release.

THE LYDIAN MODE

The fourth mode of the major scale is called the Lydian mode. (See *JPM*, page 34.) It's like a major scale, but with a raised 4th, which is usually described as the ♯11th. Here is the F Lydian mode, which is the fourth mode of the C major scale.

TRACK 234

Use the Lydian mode to improvise over major 7th chords when you want to include the ♯11th. Playing over a major 7th chord that functions as IVmaj7 is a good place to use the Lydian mode. In the following example, I improvise over Imaj7– IVmaj7–iiim7–VI7–iim7–V7–Imaj7 in the key of C. Over Fmaj7 (IVmaj7) in measure 2, I use the F Lydian mode, which essentially means staying in the key of C. When playing over IVmaj7, use the Lydian mode or simply play vocabulary that relates to Imaj7.

TRACK 235

Many modal tunes, such as "Inner Urge" by Joe Henderson, include major 7th(♯11) chords over which you can use the Lydian mode when improvising. There are no weak tones in the Lydian mode because each note functions as either a chord tone (root, 3rd, 5th, 7th) or an upper extension (9th, ♯11th, 13th) of a major 7th chord, which makes it easy to use modal patterns and lines like we did in Tracks 220-226. You can improvise over Fmaj7♯11, for example, with the same material we used that came from D Dorian, since both come from the same major scale.

To form voicings for a major 7th(♯11) chord, you can play a major 7th shell voicing or a major 7th rootless voicing with the left hand. The right hand can be used to add the ♯11th, as well as the 9th and 13th if desired. Another useful left-hand voicing can be formed by playing 1-3-♯4-7.

Here's an improvisation over Fmaj7♯11.

TRACK 236

Practice: Get familiar with the Lydian mode and improvise with it over major 7th(♯11) chords.

THE MAJOR 7th(♯5) CHORD

In *JPM*, page 17, I introduced the major 7th(♯5) chord, a major 7th chord with the 5th replaced by the raised (augmented) 5th. Imaj7♯5 is sometimes used as a substitute for Imaj7, which can be followed by I6 or IVmaj7. For example, Cmaj7♯5 might be followed by C6 or Fmaj7. In the following track, I play iim7–V7–Imaj7♯5–IVmaj7 and improvise over it. Try using this type of progression for the first half of the A section of "Autumn Leaves" or the opening four measures of the ballad, "I Fall in Love Too Easily."

TRACK 237

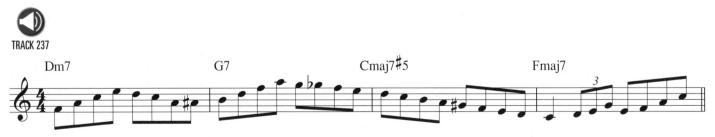

Over Cmaj7#5 on Track 237, I played a C major scale with a raised 5th, a scale called the **Ionian #5 scale**. Notice that the C Ionian #5 scale shares the same notes as an A harmonic minor scale. This is because the Ionian #5 scale is the third mode of a harmonic minor scale. Here is the C Ionian #5 scale.

Major 7th(#5) chords are often used in modern jazz tunes. In addition to the Ionian #5 scale, there are other scales that can be played over them. The third mode of the jazz melodic minor scale is one them. It is called the **Lydian augmented scale** because it's like a Lydian mode, but with a raised (augmented) 5th. Here is the C Lydian augmented scale followed by an improvisation with it over Cmaj7#5.

The **augmented scale** is another scale that can be used when improvising over a major 7th(#5) chord. It's a six-note scale that combines the notes of two augmented triads that are a minor 3rd apart, resulting in an alternating pattern of minor 3rds and half steps. Here is the C augmented scale played over Cmaj7#5. Notice that the scale contains the notes of C+ (C, E, G#) and Eb+ (Eb, G, B).

In *JPM*, pages 79-80, I explained that there are really only three diminished 7th chords and three diminished scales. A similar concept applies to augmented triads and augmented scales. Because each inversion of an augmented triad forms another root position augmented triad, it can be said that there are really only four augmented triads. Play C+, C#+, D+, and Eb+. Now play the inversions of these four triads and you will have accounted for all 12 keys. You will also find that there are only four augmented scales. Any augmented scale you play will share the same notes as one of the following four augmented scales.

The augmented scale is not used as often as the other scales I have presented, but it has a unique sound that will likely catch your ear when you hear it. Shown below is a type of augmented scale pattern you will hear Oliver Nelson play in his solo on "Stolen Moments." Freddie Hubbard also used it in his solo on "Survival of the Fittest" on Herbie Hancock's album *Maiden Voyage.* Rather than playing the augmented scale over a major 7th(#5) chord, they used it to go "outside" in their solos.

Practice: Learn to play the Ionian #5 scale, the Lydian augmented scale, and the augmented scale in all keys and improvise with them over major 7th(#5) chords.

UPPER STRUCTURE TRIADS

A triad used as the top part of a 7th-chord voicing, can be referred to as an **upper structure triad**. The most interesting and useful of these contain at least two upper extensions. They can be used with various chord qualities, but in this section we will examine their use with dominant 7th chords. Here are some examples of upper structure triads played over a C7 shell voicing. I play major triads that begin on the 9th, #11th, b13th, and 13th. I also play a minor triad that begins on the #11th, in second inversion, a common way to play this one. (Minor triads that begin on the b9th and b3rd are also useful.)

TRACK 243

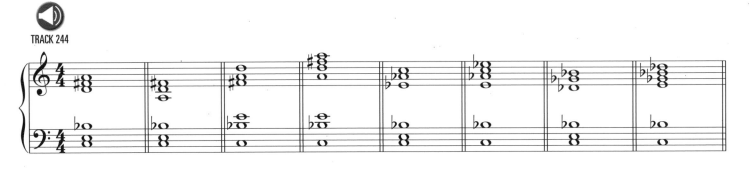

Upper structure triads can be used in root position or inverted and they can be played over a closed- or open-shell voicing. The top note of an upper structure triad can be doubled an octave below to create a big, full sound. Here are just a few examples of the many voicings that can be created using these techniques. When working with a bassist, you may choose not to play the root.

TRACK 244

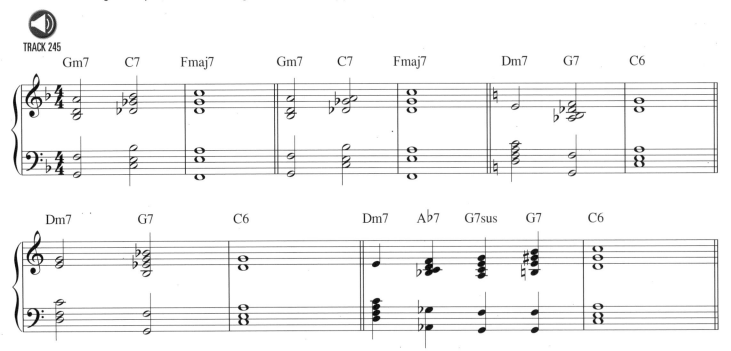

In the following example, I used voicings that include upper structure triads in ii–V–I progressions in F and C.

TRACK 245

Practice: Get familiar with the upper structure triads presented here. Include them over dominant 7th chords in iim7–V7–Imaj7s in all keys. Use them when harmonizing melodies and in your comping.

SLASH CHORDS

Many modern jazz compositions and arrangements make use of slash chords that involve a major triad played over a bass note. To acquaint yourself with the possibilities, play the following example. I ascend chromatically with triads and play a C below each chord. In the example, the triads are in root position, but they can also be played as inversions.

Some of the chord symbols from Track 246 are another way to describe a basic chord or a way to suggest a specific inversion. For example, D♭/C is an inverted D♭maj7, E♭/C is the same as Cm7, E/C is the same as Cmaj7♯5, F/C is an inverted F major triad, G/C implies Cmaj9, and B♭/C is C9sus4. D/C could be considered an inversion of D7, or it could suggest a C chord over which you would play the C Lydian mode. G♭/C, A♭/C, and A/C might be used to imply C7 chords with upper structure triads. B/C suggests C°7, over which you could play a diminished scale. You can also treat B/C as a chord that comes from E harmonic minor, so you could play the sixth mode of the harmonic minor scale over this chord.

Sometimes slash chords are part of a section of a tune that involves a **pedal point**, a note in the bass register that stays the same while chords change above it. The C you played in the left hand in Track 246 could be called a pedal point because it stays constant while chords change above it. "Cedar's Blues" by Cedar Walton is a good example of a tune that makes use of pedal points. It's common to use the tonic or a note a 5th above the tonic as a pedal point. The following example could serve as an introduction to a tune. I play iiim7–VI7–iim7–V7 twice through in the key of B♭, using rootless voicings in the right hand while playing an F pedal point on beats 2 and 4 with the left hand.

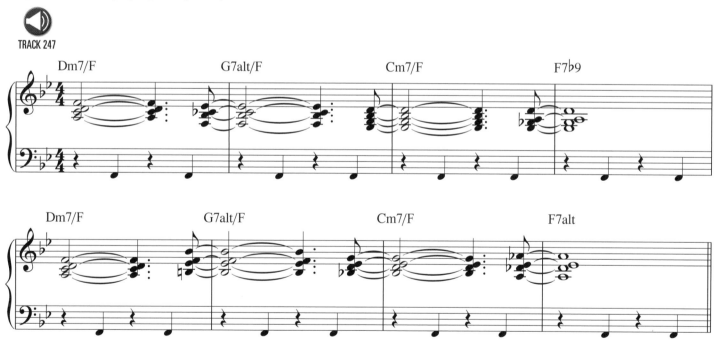

Practice: Experiment with slash chords and look for them in modern jazz compositions. See where you can make use of pedal points.

REHARMONIZATION

Throughout this book you've learned about voicings and chord substitutions you can use to harmonize or reharmonize tunes. Another method for reharmonization involves **parallel harmony**. Use identical voicings, transposed to different keys, to harmonize each note of a melody or section of a melody. In the following example, I transpose the "So What" voicing to match each note of the melody of "Happy Birthday to You." The result is a chord sequence that is determined by the contour of the melody and has nothing to do with the original harmony (which I show above the melody). Any voicing can be used to create parallel harmony.

Another method for reharmonization is **back cycling,** which involves approaching a target chord with chords that move in the order of the cycle (up in 4ths or down in 5ths). Say you want to play C as the final chord of "Happy Birthday to You," as I have done in the following example. I figured out that if I started the final phrase on B7, I can move through the cycle, matching a dominant 7th chord to each melody note and arrive at C for the last chord. Dominant 7th chords or a series of iim7–V7 progressions can work well for back cycling.

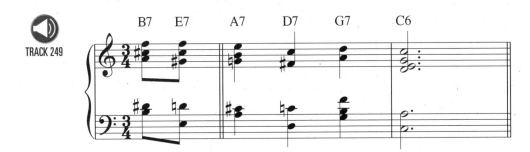

As you experiment with more adventurous reharmonization, you'll find that a chord based on any root can be used to harmonize any melody note. This simply requires using a chord quality that works with the particular melody note. To start exploring more unusual ways to reharmonize a tune, try voicing the first note of a phrase based on an arbitrary root. To create a direction for the root movement as you proceed through the song, try ascending or descending chromatically or with other intervals. Experiment with different starting points and different root movements until you find something you like.

In the following example, I reharmonized the opening of "Happy Birthday to You." I arbitrarily started on B7 and continued with a root movement that descends chromatically until the last two measures where I used parallel voicings.

For the final example, I reharmonized "Danny Boy" using many of the harmonic techniques presented in this book. The basic chords used as a starting point are shown in italics above the chords of the reharmonization. Among the many techniques used, you'll find parallel harmony in measures 18, 20-21, and 29-31, and back cycling in measures 4 and 26. In measures 16 and 24, I used an arbitrary starting point and descended chromatically.

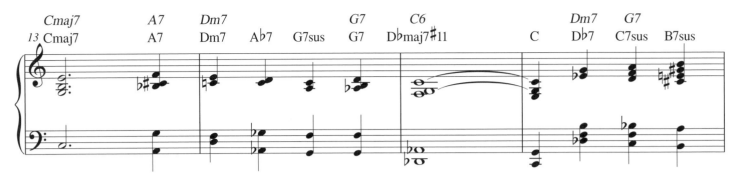

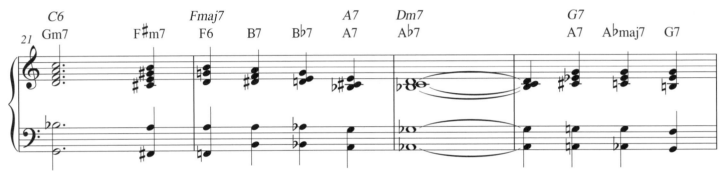

Practice: Select a favorite tune and reharmonize it using techniques presented in this section. Come up with other reharmonizations of the same tune.

CONCLUSION

I hope this book inspired you and helped cultivate your creativity. Both this book and *JPM* are resources you can refer to often and use to structure your practice. Learning to play jazz piano can be overwhelming – there are so many tunes to learn, solos to transcribe, and techniques to practice. Just take things one step at a time and know that you are fortunate to be involved in such a fascinating endeavor. Keep going because new discoveries await you. Even in his 90s, jazz piano master Hank Jones was still practicing several hours a day. He felt he had yet to give his best performance.

GLOSSARY

Here are brief definitions of terms that appeared in bold throughout this book. See the glossary in *JPM* for the meanings of additional musical terms.

Afro-Caribbean music: An umbrella term for various African-influenced music styles of the Caribbean.

atonal: Without a key or tonal center.

augmented scale: A six-note scale that combines the notes of two augmented triads that are a minor 3rd apart, resulting in an alternating pattern of minor 3rds and half steps.

back cycling: Approaching a target chord with chords that move in the order of the cycle (up in 4ths or down in 5ths).

Bird: Charlie Parker's nickname. He was also known as Yardbird.

bitonality: The use of two different key centers at the same time.

block chords: Voicings used to harmonize a melody or solo line that involve both hands playing the same rhythm.

chops: Technical proficiency on a musical instrument.

chord substitution (chord sub): A chord used in place of another chord in a progression.

chord tone: A note within a chord.

chromatic approach chord: A chord that ascends or descends by a half step to lead to another chord.

chromatic approach note: A note that ascends or descends by a half step to lead to a target note.

clave: A repeated two-bar rhythmic pattern used in various types of Latin American music.

closed voicing (a.k.a. close or closed position voicing): A voicing that fits within the span of an octave.

Coltrane cycle (a.k.a. Coltrane changes): A harmonic progression that John Coltrane used to compose and reharmonize tunes. It involves three major 7th chords that descend in major 3rds, each preceded by its V7.

drop-two voicing: A voicing created from a four-note closed position voicing by shifting the second note from the top down an octave.

four-note closed position voicing (a.k.a. four-way close voicing): A four-note chord voiced within the span of an octave.

4th voicing: A chord voiced using 4th intervals.

guajeo: See montuno

guide tone: Typically, the 3rd or 7th of a chord.

guide tone line: Melody composed of guide tones.

harmonic rhythm: The rate at which chords change in a given progression.

Ionian ♯5 scale: The third mode of a harmonic minor scale.

locked-hands style: A type of block chording in which the pianist plays both hands together as if in handcuffs.

Locrian ♮2 scale: The sixth mode of a jazz melodic minor scale.

Lydian augmented scale: The third mode of a jazz melodic minor scale.

Lydian dominant scale: The fourth mode of a jazz melodic minor scale.

major pentatonic scale: A five-note scale composed of the first, second, third, fifth, and sixth degrees of a major scale.

major 6th-diminished scale: A scale that contains the four notes of a major 6th chord and the four notes of a diminished 7th chord a half step below.

minor 6th-diminished scale: A scale that contains the four notes of a minor 6th chord and the four notes of a diminished 7th chord a half step below.

modal jazz: A compositional style that emerged in the 1950s that uses modes as the basis for chords, melodies, and improvisations. Typically, these pieces include long stretches based on a particular mode. Chords in modal tunes often move in nontraditional ways.

montuno (a.k.a. guajeo): A repeated figure typically played by the pianist in much Afro-Cuban music.

open voicing (a.k.a. open position voicing): A voicing that spans more than an octave.

parallel harmony: Two or more identical voicings played in different keys that are used in succession.

passing chord: A chord inserted between two chords in a progression to create harmonic interest.

pedal point (a.k.a. pedal tone or pedal): A note in the bass register that stays the same while chords change above it.

pivoting: Barry Harris's term for shifting up an octave during a descending scale run.

quartal harmony: A system that involves chords formed by stacking 4ths.

reharmonize: Replace the original chords of a passage or song with different ones.

resolve: Move melodically or harmonically from dissonance to consonance.

retrograde: A series of notes played backward.

run: An ascending or descending line that typically covers several octaves.

salsa: Popular dance music that developed in New York City in the 1960s based on Afro-Cuban and Puerto Rican styles.

samba: A Brazilian style of music and dance.

scalar: From a scale.

secondary dominant: A dominant 7th chord that resolves down a 5th (up a 4th) to a chord other than the tonic chord.

stepwise: Moving by adjacent scale tones rather than larger intervals.

surround tones: Notes that are diatonically or chromatically adjacent to a target note used in an enclosure.

target note: A chord tone or other note to which a melodic figure leads.

tertian harmony: A system that involves chords formed by stacking 3rds.

tonic chord: A chord formed on the tonic (first degree) of a scale.

Trane: John Coltrane's nickname.

tritone substitution (tritone sub): Replacement of a dominant 7th chord with another dominant 7th chord that is a tritone (three whole steps) away.

upper structure triad: A triad used as the top part of a 7th-chord voicing.

vamp: A musical figure based on one or a limited number of repeated chords, used as a solo section, intro, or ending. This term can also be used as a verb meaning: Play a repeated figure until cue.

walking bass line: A continuous series of low-register quarter notes, with occasional rhythmic embellishments, composed of roots and other notes related to the harmony of the tune.

walking 10ths: Ascending or descending quarter-note lines played in 10ths by a pianist's left hand.

TRACK LISTING

Track titles in bold are performed by a trio.
All other tracks are solo piano (except Tracks 198–199, which are percussion only).

Mark Davis – piano
Jeff Hamann – bass
David Bayles – drums

Recorded by Ric Probst at Tanner-Monagle Studio, Milwaukee, WI.

Chapter 1: Strengthening the Basics

1. Closed-shell voicing (p. 5)
2. Various chord qualities played with closed-shell voicings (p. 6)
3. Various chord qualities played with open-shell voicings (p. 6)
4. Closed-shell voicings with one or two notes added (p. 6)
5. Open-shell voicings with one or two notes added (p. 7)
6. Major 7th, four-note, two-handed voicing exercise (p. 8)
7. Major 7th, four-note, two-handed voicing exercise up a half step (p. 8)
8. **Major 7th, four-note, two-handed voicing exercise with comping rhythms** (p. 8)
9. Minor 7th, four-note, two-handed voicing exercise (p. 9)
10. Minor 7th, four-note, two-handed voicing exercise up a half step (p. 9)
11. Dominant 7th, four-note, two-handed voicing exercise (p. 9)
12. Dominant 7th, four-note, two-handed voicing exercise up a half step (p. 10)
13. Four-note, two-handed voicing exercise that alternates between adding the ♭13th and the 9th to dominant 7th chords (p. 10)
14. Four-note, two-handed voicing exercise that alternates between adding the ♭13th and the ♯9th to dominant 7th chords (p. 10)
15. Four-note, two-handed voicing exercise that alternates between adding the 5th and the ♭9th to dominant 7th chords (p. 10)
16. Four-note, two-handed voicing exercise that alternates between adding the 5th and the ♯9th to dominant 7th chords (p. 11)
17. Major 7th, five-note, two-handed voicing exercise (p. 11)
18. Another major 7th, five-note, two-handed voicing exercise (p. 11)
19. Minor 7th, five-note, two-handed voicing exercise (p. 11)
20. Another minor 7th, five-note, two-handed voicing exercise (p. 12)
21. Dominant 7th, five-note, two-handed voicing exercise (p. 12)
22. Another dominant 7th, five-note, two-handed voicing exercise (p. 12)
23. Dominant 7th, five-note, two-handed voicing exercise that includes altered extensions (p. 12)
24. Another dominant 7th, five-note, two-handed voicing exercise that includes altered extensions (p. 13)
25. One more dominant 7th, five-note, two-handed voicing exercise that includes altered extensions (p. 13)
26. Five-note voicings applied to a iim7–V7–Imaj7 progression (p. 13)
27. Dominant 7th voicings with altered extensions included in the iim7–V7–Imaj7 progression (p. 13)
28. Guide tone line through the cycle (p. 14)
29. Scale ideas (p. 14)
30. Line over a cycle of dominant 7th chords (p. 15)
31. Chord tone ideas (p. 15)
32. Another line over a cycle of dominant 7th chords (p. 15)
33. Guide tone line over a progression (p. 15)

Chapter 2: Expanding Your Melodic Vocabulary

34. Three four-note arpeggios connected by a dominant scale (p. 16)
35. Extended arpeggios (p. 16)
36. Arpeggio from the 3rd of G7 with a leap to the 13th (p. 16)
37. Reverse direction arpeggios (p. 17)
38. Reverse direction arpeggios connected to scales (p. 17)
39. Scale with 16th-note embellishments (p. 17)
40. Scale with embellishments that use 16th-note triplets (p. 17)
41. Bebop scales with embellishments on chord tones (p. 18)
42. Improvisation with embellishments (p. 18)
43. Phrase over iim7–V7–Imaj7 (p. 18)
44. Embellishments that begin on upper extensions (p. 18)
45. Descending melodic intervals and descending arpeggios with embellishments (p. 19)
46. Enclosure that targets the 3rd of the G7 scale (p. 19)
47. Idea that includes an enclosure that targets the 3rd of the G7 scale (p. 19)
48. Enclosure with surround tones reversed that targets the 3rd of the G7 scale (p. 19)
49. Ideas that include an enclosure with surround tones reversed that target the 3rd of the G7 scale (p. 20)
50. **Melodic line that includes enclosures that target the 3rd of the G7 scale** (p. 20)
51. Enclosure that targets the 7th of the G7 scale (p. 20)
52. Idea that includes an enclosure that targets the 7th of the G7 scale (p. 20)
53. Enclosure with the surround tones reversed that targets the 7th of the G7 scale (p. 20)
54. Ideas that include an enclosure with the surround tones reversed that target the 7th of the G7 scale (p. 20)
55. **Melodic line that includes enclosures that target the 7th of the G7 scale** (p. 21)
56. Enclosure idea that targets the third and second notes of the G7 scale (p. 21)
57. **Melodic line that includes an enclosure that targets the third and second notes of the G7 scale** (p. 21)
58. Enclosures that target the fifth of the G7 scale (p. 21)
59. Dominant arpeggios followed by enclosures that target the fifth of the G7 scale (p. 21)
60. More dominant ideas that include enclosures that target the fifth of the G7 scale (p. 22)
61. **Melodic line that includes enclosure ideas that target the fifth of a dominant scale** (p. 22)
62. Dominant enclosures preceded by chromatic approach notes that start on upbeats (p. 22)
63. Back-to-back dominant enclosures with chromatic approach notes (p. 22)
64. Phrases that use dominant enclosures with chromatic approach notes that start on upbeats (p. 22)
65. Dominant enclosures preceded by chromatic approach notes that start on the beat (p. 23)
66. Phrases that include dominant enclosures preceded by chromatic approach notes that start on the beat (p. 23)
67. Targeting the third and first notes of a dominant 7th scale with the lower surround note raised (p. 23)
68. Enclosures that target the root, 3rd, and 5th of a major chord (p. 23)
69. Phrases that include enclosures that target the root, 3rd, and 5th of a major chord (p. 23)

Chapter 3: Chord Progressions and Substitutions

Chapter 4: Jazz Melodic Minor Scale Theory

Chapter 5: Movable Voicings and Accompaniment Styles

ACKNOWLEDGMENTS

Special thanks to Erin, my family, friends, and former teachers, for your support and guidance, and to my students, past and present, for inspiring me to continue learning. In particular, I would like to thank my good friend Rick Krause for his invaluable help with this book.

ABOUT THE AUTHOR

Mark Davis is an accomplished pianist and an influential educator who has performed with jazz luminaries Eric Alexander, Peter Bernstein, Benny Golson, Slide Hampton, Tom Harrell, Jimmy Heath, Brian Lynch, Charles McPherson, Frank Morgan, and Phil Woods, among others.

Mark began piano studies at age eight and soon took to improvising and composing. His teachers included Adelaide Banaszynski and David Hazeltine. He later studied with jazz legend Barry Harris, who remains one of Mark's primary inspirations as a player and educator.

Mark taught at the Wisconsin Conservatory of Music and served as chair of the jazz department for 27 years. He founded the Milwaukee Jazz Institute in 2019 and serves as artistic director. He also teaches privately and is on the music faculty of Alverno College. Many of Mark's former students have gone on to successful careers in music, most notably Dan Nimmer, pianist with Wynton Marsalis and the Jazz at Lincoln Center Orchestra.

Mark's previous work for Hal Leonard includes authoring the *Hal Leonard Jazz Piano Method* and making numerous recordings for their *Real Book Play-Along* series and *Real Book Multi-Tracks* series.

For more information, visit www.markdavismusic.com.

PLAY PIANO LIKE A PRO!

AMAZING PHRASING – KEYBOARD
50 Ways to Improve Your Improvisational Skills
by Debbie Denke

Amazing Phrasing is for any keyboard player interested in learning how to improvise and how to improve their creative phrasing. This method is divided into three parts: melody, harmony, and rhythm & style. The online audio contains 44 full-band demos for listening, as well as many play-along examples so you can practice improvising over various musical styles and progressions.
00842030 Book/Online Audio... $16.99

BEBOP LICKS FOR PIANO
A Dictionary of Melodic Ideas for Improvisation
by Les Wise

Written for the musician who is interested in acquiring a firm foundation for playing jazz, this unique book/audio pack presents over 800 licks. By building up a vocabulary of these licks, players can connect them together in endless possibilities to form larger phrases and complete solos. The book includes piano notation, and the online audio contains helpful note-for-note demos of every lick.
00311854 Book/Online Audio... $17.99

BOOGIE WOOGIE FOR BEGINNERS
by Frank Paparelli

A short easy method for learning to play boogie woogie, designed for the beginner and average pianist. Includes: exercises for developing left-hand bass • 25 popular boogie woogie bass patterns • arrangements of "Down the Road a Piece" and "Answer to the Prayer" by well-known pianists • a glossary of musical terms for dynamics, tempo and style.
00120517 .... $10.99

HAL LEONARD JAZZ PIANO METHOD
by Mark Davis

This is a comprehensive and easy-to-use guide designed for anyone interested in playing jazz piano – from the complete novice just learning the basics to the more advanced player who wishes to enhance their keyboard vocabulary. The accompanying audio includes demonstrations of all the examples in the book! Topics include essential theory, chords and voicings, improvisation ideas, structure and forms, scales and modes, rhythm basics, interpreting a lead sheet, playing solos, and much more!
00131102 Book/Online Audio... $19.99

INTROS, ENDINGS & TURNAROUNDS FOR KEYBOARD
Essential Phrases for Swing, Latin, Jazz Waltz, and Blues Styles
by John Valerio

Learn the intros, endings and turnarounds that all of the pros know and use! This new keyboard instruction book by John Valerio covers swing styles, ballads, Latin tunes, jazz waltzes, blues, major and minor keys, vamps and pedal tones, and more.
00290525 .... $12.99

JAZZ PIANO TECHNIQUE
Exercises, Etudes & Ideas for Building Chops
by John Valerio

This one-of-a-kind book applies traditional technique exercises to specific jazz piano needs. Topics include: scales (major, minor, chromatic, pentatonic, etc.), arpeggios (triads, seventh chords, upper structures), finger independence exercises (static position, held notes, Hanon exercises), parallel interval scales and exercises (thirds, fourths, tritones, fifths, sixths, octaves), and more! The online audio includes 45 recorded examples.
00312059 Book/Online Audio... $19.99

JAZZ PIANO VOICINGS
An Essential Resource for Aspiring Jazz Musicians
by Rob Mullins

The jazz idiom can often appear mysterious and difficult for musicians who were trained to play other types of music. Long-time performer and educator Rob Mullins helps players enter the jazz world by providing voicings that will help the player develop skills in the jazz genre and start sounding professional right away – without years of study! Includes a "Numeric Voicing Chart," chord indexes in all 12 keys, info about what range of the instrument you can play chords in, and a beginning approach to bass lines.
00310914 .... $19.99

OSCAR PETERSON – JAZZ EXERCISES, MINUETS, ETUDES & PIECES FOR PIANO

Legendary jazz pianist Oscar Peterson has long been devoted to the education of piano students. In this book he offers dozens of pieces designed to empower the student, whether novice or classically trained, with the technique needed to become an accomplished jazz pianist.
00311225 .... $14.99

PIANO AEROBICS
by Wayne Hawkins

Piano Aerobics is a set of exercises that introduces students to many popular styles of music, including jazz, salsa, swing, rock, blues, new age, gospel, stride, and bossa nova. In addition, there is a online audio with accompaniment tracks featuring professional musicians playing in those styles.
00311863 Book/Online Audio..................... $19.99

PIANO FITNESS
A Complete Workout
by Mark Harrison

This book will give you a thorough technical workout, while having fun at the same time! The accompanying online audio allows you to play along with a rhythm section as you practice your scales, arpeggios, and chords in all keys. Instead of avoiding technique exercises because they seem too tedious or difficult, you'll look forward to playing them. Various voicings and rhythmic settings, which are extremely useful in a variety of pop and jazz styles, are also introduced.
00311995 Book/Online Audio... $19.99

HAL•LEONARD®
7777 W. BLUEMOUND RD. P.O. BOX 13819
MILWAUKEE, WISCONSIN 53213
www.halleonard.com

Prices, contents, and availability subject to change without notice.

TESTIMONIALS

"Mark Davis has done it again! His easy-to-read examples enable the reader to play authentic, relevant jazz lines and chord progressions immediately. Mark masterfully presents the most useful elements of jazz piano language in a clear and concise way. This is a must-have text for students and teachers alike!"

—Steve Allee, Grammy®-nominated pianist
(has worked with Randy Brecker, John Clayton, David "Fathead" Newman, Rufus Reid, Buddy Rich, and others)

"Mark Davis's *Jazz Piano Method Book 2* and his earlier *Jazz Piano Method* are outstanding books for all aspiring jazz pianists. Mark is a superb pianist and educator who possesses the rare ability to explain and organize concepts in a way that is clear, logical, and easy to follow. These books are comprehensive and cover a wide range of essential information, presented in a way that makes learning jazz improvisation accessible to musicians of all experience levels. I recommend *Jazz Piano Method* and *Jazz Piano Method Book 2* to all of my students at the University of North Florida."

—Lynne Arriale, pianist and Professor of Jazz Studies and Director of Small Ensembles at the University of North Florida
(has worked with Randy Brecker, Benny Golson, George Mraz, and others)

"This is a powerhouse of a book—a real 'owner's manual' for the jazz piano mind. Mark Davis presents the essential material in easily digestible packets, each building on the last, and as a whole building on the concepts from the first book. I'll be referring both beginning and intermediate students to this course."

—Geoffrey Keezer, multiple Grammy®-nominated pianist
(has worked with Art Blakey and the Jazz Messengers, Chris Botti, Ray Brown, Art Farmer, Benny Golson, Joe Locke, Christian McBride, Dianne Reeves, David Sanborn, Wayne Shorter, Sting, and others)

"Mark Davis does it again with this extremely informative, accurate, and fun approach to learning jazz piano. This book is a great way to learn from a true master of this music who mentored me and helped me become the musician I am today."

—Dan Nimmer, pianist with Wynton Marsalis and the Jazz at Lincoln Center Orchestra
(has worked with Rubén Blades, Eric Clapton, Jimmy Cobb, Chick Corea, Norah Jones, Willie Nelson, Paul Simon, and others)

"In the many years that I have known Mark Davis, he has always held himself to a high standard as musician and educator. It is no surprise then, that he should write such comprehensible and thorough jazz piano method books. *Book 2* is a wealth of knowledge, reinforcing and augmenting information from his previous volume. I love both of these books and plan to use them regularly with my students."

—Gregory Tardy, Associate Professor of Jazz Saxophone at the University of Tennessee, Knoxville
(has worked with Bill Frisell, Andrew Hill, Elvin Jones, Brian Lynch, Wynton Marsalis, and others)